THE BEST BOOK OF BIZARRE BUT TRUE STORIES... EVER!

This is a Carlton book

This edition published 1999 by Carlton Books Limited, 20 St Anne's Court, Wardour Street, London W1V 3AW

ISBN 1 85868 558 3

Printed and bound in Great Britain

The names of some people and places in this book have been changed to protect identities.

THE BEST BOOK OF BIZARRE BUT TRUE STORIES... EVER!

Mike Flynn

CARLTON

CONTENTS

ACCIDENTS

There is something funny about the sight of someone we don't know injuring themselves as a result of their own foolishness. Quite possibly the only thing that could be funnier is the sight of someone we do know doing the same thing. I almost blush with shame at the memory of laughing uncontrollably when, as a child, my brother fell off a statue of Oliver Cromwell and broke his arm as he hit the ground. For me it was a classic example of life imitating art – in this case the art of slapstick. The fact that slapstick humour is so predictable is what makes it so appealing; there is an inevitability about it that is almost reassuring. Coupled with the easy appeal of slapstick is a factor in the human psyche which runs far deeper than simple comedy. As a species we have a cruel streak which has given us a winning edge in our battle for survival but which also finds an outlet in the things we find funny. As a result, the line between tragedy and comedy is so fine as to be almost non-existent. After all, who among us would not collapse with laughter at the sight of the Queen falling backwards off her horse during Trooping the Colour – always assuming, of course, that she didn't hurt herself?

BUGGED OUT

A man in California, US, became so frustrated with the number of bugs in his apartment that he decided to take drastic action. Arming himself with eight 'Bug Bombs' – explosive devices designed to spread insecticide over a wide area – he sat and waited for the insects to put in an appearance. Unfortunately, he had not read the packaging, which warned that no more than one device should be used at a time, and that a detonation should never, ever, happen in a confined space. The explosion that resulted from all eight devices going off at once blew him out of his apartment, started a fire and caused structural damage to the entire building. A number of bugs were also hurt.

BLEEDING BOOZER

The phrase 'dying for a drink' took on a whole new meaning during last year's beer festival in Munich, Germany. It's not unusual for people to drink each other under the table during festivities, but for one man things got more than a little out of hand. As he slid into oblivion he took his beer glass with him, smashing it on the way down and slicing open an artery in his neck. "We thought he was messing around", slurred one bystander, "until someone slipped up on the blood and realized what was going on". The fortunate victim made a complete recovery and, proving that you can't keep a good man down, was back at the festival by the end of the week.

HOLE IN ONE

Malaysians are renowned the world over for their exquisite manners, so it should come as no surprise to hear of a golfing businessman who had the misfortune to be standing too close as his partner played the ball. The businessman was caught around the back of the head by his partner's powerful backswing and went crashing to the ground. Almost immediately, the businessman leapt to his feet, apologized profusely to his partner for impeding his stroke, and then promptly dropped down dead. His partner was judged to have won the round by default.

RACOON BOOM

A man from Pennsylvania was sitting on his back porch drinking beer with his red-neck friends when he spotted a racoon. In true "you ain't from 'round these parts, boy" fashion he reached for his gun. Dodging a fusillade of some 40 shots, the animal was able to escape, unharmed, into a drainage pipe. Not one to give up easily, the man emptied the entire contents of a five-gallon can of gasoline down the pipe before climbing into it to set the fuel alight (in the hope of smoking the animal out). The resulting explosion blew the man out of the hole and over the top of his own house. Interviewed later, the man said that he felt the whole experience was "pretty cool" and that he'd do it again if he could be sure he would be unhurt.

WASH AND... GONE

A tragic tale was reported in Bombay, where an eight-year-old boy accidentally killed his younger brother by washing him in a washing machine. The boy had been inspired to clean his brother in this way after watching a TV commercial in which a very grubby teddy bear was transformed as the result of going through a full automatic wash cycle.

FALL-OUT

Feeling unlucky? Well spare a thought for a Brazilian woman who had the great misfortune to be killed in someone else's air crash. Two planes collided in mid-air during an anniversary event at a local airport. The un-named woman, although standing under the collision, managed to avoid the falling debris and burning fuel. However, she was unlucky enough to be squashed under a falling body. The accident investigator blamed the collision on pilot error, but the woman's death may be chalked up to an Act of God.

LOBSTER'S REVENGE

Anyone who claims that today's men have been softened up by too much good living have obviously never heard the tale of the lobster fisherman whose arm became caught in a moving winch on his boat. Faced with the choice of being pulled bodily into the machinery or simply losing his arm, the 33-year-old fisherman quite sensibly opted for the latter. The only question was: how was he going to separate himself from his arm? Most people might have paused at this point, but our hero simply pulled out his pocket knife and began to hack away. In no time at all he was free of the machinery although a little short in the limb department.

POLISH CHAINSAW MASSACRE

A Polish farmer who was determined to prove that, despite the fact that he wore his sister's underwear, he was far more macho than most, went somewhat further than his audience anticipated in order to prove his point. After having more than a few drinks with his friends, he suggested that they all strip naked and play "men's games". This is believed to have involved hitting each other over the head with frozen swedes. Having tired of this (all good things must come to an end) the farmer picked up a chainsaw and swung it above his head before bringing it around one last time and decapitating himself.

SELF-BUILD KILLED

A 71-year-old pensioner from San Francisco realized his life's ambition when he finally took off in an aeroplane that he had built himself. The pensioner had spent 18 years building the aircraft in his garage and chose the Experimental Aircraft Association Exhibition in Wisconsin for the plane's maiden flight. After a thorough inspection by the Federal Aviation Administration, the retired engineer took to the air, for a few seconds. The poor man had barely cleared the runway when his engine seized up, causing the plane to crash and kill him instantly.

LEGAL EAGLE PLUMMETS

Police in Canada were deeply dismayed when they discovered that a lawyer by the name of Garry Hoy, one of the best and brightest attorneys with the firm Holden Day Wilson, had died not so much by accident as by sheer stupidity. The 39-year-old had plummeted to his death after choosing to demonstrate the strength of his office windows to a group of visiting law students. Rather than tap the window with a heavy object, Hoy charged shoulder first at it and fell 24 floors to the ground when the window broke.

DEATH BY DOG

A man in St Louis, behaving in a disorderly and offensive manner, was approached by a shop assistant and asked to leave the store. Robert Puelo, 32, refused and when the assistant threatened to call the police, Puelo grabbed a hot dog and attempted to swallow it whole before leaving the store without paying. Alas, he did not get very far. When the police arrived at the store they found him dead on the pavement. Cause of death was given as "choking on a six-inch hot dog".

SODA SQUASH

In what sounds suspiciously like an episode of The Simpsons, an American man was crushed to death by a Coke machine. Apparently, he had been trying to reach inside the machine in order to steal a can of Coke. Remarkably, he had managed to reach the can, but was having difficulty removing it from the machine. Deciding that all that was needed was brute force, the man pulled with all his might, only to overbalance the machine and pull it down on top of himself. According to police reports, the man died with $3 in change and $25 in notes in his pockets.

BRIGHT SPARKS

It appears these days that no matter how secure business premises are, there are some villains who simply cannot be guarded against. A gang of burglars attempted to break into a fireworks factory in Kent, England, but made a fundamental error when it came to making their entry. Rather than using something sensible, like a crowbar, to force open the doors, they decided to cut their way in using an oxy-acetylene blowtorch. Despite the fact that the factory was a former World-War-Two ammunition dump, with foot-thick stone walls, it was reduced to rubble by the inevitable explosion caused by the meeting of flame and fireworks. The blast was heard five miles away; police have yet to find the bodies of the raiders.

PASTA BLASTER

Fate can be horribly cruel at times. Take the case of the 42-year-old Italian kitchen worker who decided to end it all after becoming convinced that his wife no longer loved him. He decided to blow his brains out with his father's old wartime revolver but, just as he was about to pull the trigger, his wife burst in and begged him to put the gun down. He was reluctant to do so at first but after much discussion and many, many reassurances his wife was able to convince the man that she did still love him as much as she had on the day they married. Realizing his foolishness, he threw the gun down and moved to embrace his wife. Unfortunately, as the old revolver hit the floor it went off, killing his wife instantly.

TREE CHOPS DOWN MAN

Sometimes it's just not your day. This was certainly the case for 55-year-old Caesar Vittoro, an Italian motorist who had the great misfortune to be out driving near Naples, Italy, during a storm. A powerful gust of wind blew his speeding car off a bridge and into a river. The river, which was by now a raging torrent because of the tremendous storm, all but sucked the car under. Fortunately, brave Caesar was able to smash a window and battle his way across the water to the safety of the river bank… where the wind blew a tree straight down on his head, crushing his skull in an instant.

LAST BLAST

We can all find it in our hearts to pity the factory owner who just managed to escape with his life when his fireworks factory exploded. Fortunately for most of the staff, the factory was being given its yearly deep cleaning and so they were at home when the explosion occurred. The factory owner, Mr John Downes, was treated for burns and a broken arm but was able to return to the factory the next day. He was greatly disappointed to discover that all that remained of his premises was a single 12-foot wall, against which was leaning one charred filing cabinet. Mr Downes opened the cabinet in order to find out what it contained, but in doing so disturbed the unstable wall, which collapsed and killed him instantly.

SAD, BUT TRUE

Yet more people have died in America as a result of what can best be described as the lethal but amusing combination of stupidity and cruel fate. Two friends, who were competing to see who would be the last to jump out of the way of a moving train, died after they both left it too late. The driver of the train, who had to be treated for shock and sheer incredulity, said that as he approached the men he had assumed that they would get out of the way. He was travelling at just 12 mph at the time, but realized too late that they had probably been drinking. Almost at the same time as that incident was occurring, a man in Chicago was drowning in 14 inches of water after sticking his head between the bars of a drainage grate in order to retrieve his car keys and then getting stuck just as the heavens opened. His wife said later that the manner of her husband's death had led her to believe that God had sent for one of his own.

BOGGED DOWN

Oh, what it is to be born lucky! In September 1994, Sharon McClelland jumped out of an aeroplane at high altitude in the name of sport and fun. Unfortunately for her, when the time came to open the parachute and enjoy the view, hers failed to open. Fortune was, however, smiling on Ms McClelland that day, for although she hit the ground without managing to open her back-up parachute, she landed relatively softly in a shallow marsh. Most people would have stayed on the ground at this point, but Ms McClelland is made of sterner stuff. She simply apologized to her instructor for not following correct procedure in a no-open situation and then headed off to make another jump.

BOLT FROM THE BREW

The Mountain Men Anonymous club is a group made up of...anonymous mountain men. They are a select band who seek to become at one with nature and get back to the simple, honest lifestyle of the great backwoods men of American folklore. As part of the initiation into the group, a man must stand with a beer can on his head while an established member takes a shot at knocking it off with a crossbow. Unfortunately for the initiate in this story, the group had decided to hold the celebration of initiation before the actual event. Most of the men there had already consumed around 16 cans of beer each when the shot was taken. The bolt from the crossbow shot through the initiate's left eye and ploughed through several inches of brain before coming to rest sticking out on the other side of his head. Incredibly, the would-be mountain man suffered no permanent brain damage and was released from hospital after just a few days sporting a remarkably life-like glass eye and a Mountain Men Anonymous membership tag.

AVOIDABLE DEATHS

There's nothing funny about death but there are some people who ought to have been made saints after they died, if only as a reward for being kind enough to die in an entertaining way. Two prime candidates for sainthood would have to be the Canadian men who died as a result of playing chicken in their snowmobiles. Despite the fact that neither vehicle was capable of travelling at more than 20 mph, the men died in a head-on collision after both refused to back down. Meanwhile, a jogger in San Francisco died after forgetting to make a left turn and instead running straight off a 200-foot cliff. His wife said later that he was "totally focused when he ran". Not on the road unfortunately. And finally, there is the case of the young boy cut down tragically early in life after he died from a fall while swinging on a sign erected to draw attention to the danger at a spot where a man had previously fallen to his death.

TOURIST ATTRACTION

Canada can offer some astonishing attractions for the kind of tourist who loves to look at scenery. The landscape is often rendered all the more dramatic by a light covering of snow, which seems to bring out the best in any stretch of countryside. Unfortunately, snow can also be a source of danger, as one tourist discovered when approaching a waterfall in a well-known beauty spot. The beauty of the waterfall was such that he was not paying attention to where he was stepping. Slipping on some snow, he plunged headfirst over the end of a cliff and crashed to his death on the rocks near the base of the waterfall. Unfortunately, his body proved difficult to recover and it was several days before rescue teams could recover it. In the meantime, local traders noticed an increase in business as a new kind of morbid, rubbernecking tourist arrived to check out the latest attraction at the waterfall.

BATHROOM BOOM

Sometimes the obvious solution to a problem is not always the one that springs immediately to mind – and sometimes the most sane and rational among us can behave in ways that can only be described as truly deranged. A prime example of this is the case of a man from Wood Green, one of the leafiest and most attractive parts of London, England. Discovering that his young son had jammed a bath sponge down the toilet, Dad attempted to dislodge it by covering it with – what else? – 3 gallons of petrol. The fumes from the petrol were ignited by the pilot light in a water heater that was situated in the bathroom, causing an explosion that ripped out most of the bathroom. There were no injuries, but from what little remained of the toilet, it was clear that more than petrol was needed to move the sponge.

TEXAN EXITS

Two tragic deaths took place in Texas after what appears to be a failure to understand the nature of guns and just what it is that they are designed to do. While sitting out on his back porch, a former war veteran noticed a large fly crawling up his leg, over-reacted, reached for his shotgun and proceeded to blow away the fly. Unfortunately the wound to his leg was so severe that he bled to death before paramedics could reach him. In the same State, and at practically the same time, a man died in Austin (the city where all the good country singers come from) after he started a game of Russian roulette using a semi-automatic weapon and forgot to take his finger off the trigger after the first shot.

DENTAL DOOM

Many people quite rightly consider a trip to the dentist to be one of the scariest experiences that life can offer. No one who has ever seen the demented figure of Laurence Olivier in Marathon Man, demanding to know "Is it safe?" while shoving a drill into the freshly split tooth of Dustin Hoffman, will ever feel the same way again about going for a filling. So it is not all that surprising that when Walter Hallas, a 26-year-old store worker from Leeds, was suffering from a toothache he requested that a friend smack him in the jaw in the hope of loosening the tooth and saving him a trip to the dentist. Unfortunately for Mr Hallas, his friend's punch was so hard that he fell to the floor, where he fractured his skull and died.

CROSSING CHAOS

A motorcyclist was travelling through Europe when he came to a railway crossing. The gates were down and so he waited for the train to pass. While he was waiting, a local villager came along with a goat in tow. He tied the goat to the crossing gate, smiled at the motorcyclist and together they waited for the train to pass. A few moments later, another villager arrived driving a horse and cart, then a man in a sports car arrived to join the queue. All was fine until an express train came screaming through the crossing, startling the horse. The horse reared up and bit the motorcyclist on the arm. The motorcyclist responded by punching the horse on the nose. Not one to tolerate the abuse of animals, the horse's owner got down off his cart and punched the motorcyclist. The ensuing fight alarmed the horse all the more – so much so that it tried to retreat from the fight but instead succeeded merely in crashing the cart into the sports car. The driver of the sports car leapt from his vehicle and joined in the fight. At this point, the man with the goat attempted to intervene and calm things down. While he was doing so, he failed to notice the crossing gates lifting and his goat being strangled.

DYING FOR A CIGARETTE

Some people just don't know when to give up smoking. No matter how many set backs they get, they continue to line the pockets of the caring, sharing tobacco companies. One such man was 64-year-old Fred Langton of Oldham, a town in the north of England. After a smoking-related cancer threatened to end his life, Mr Langton underwent surgery on his throat that robbed him of the power of speech. Despite this, he continued to smoke. Convalescing at his home and unable to find any matches or a cigarette lighter, Mr Langton attempted to light his cigarette from a gas cooker. Unfortunately, one end of the bandage around his throat had worked loose and caught fire on the cooker. The flames spread quickly to his clothes before setting furniture alight. Mr Langton might have been able to escape the blaze had he been able to call for help, but because of his recent surgery, he was unable to do so.

MIND YOUR HEADS...

It's always sad when a young life is wasted, torn from this world before it has been given the opportunity to make any real contribution. With this thought in mind, a company in Newport, South Wales, took it on themselves to produce a series of safety films warning against the many dangers that face us all in the modern world. A young actor called Lucian Lockeheart was chosen to warn of the dangers of low-level bridges. The opening shot of the film required young Lucian to travel on an open-top bus as it approached just such a bridge. He was required to utter the line "Do you know the height of your vehicle?" before ducking as the bus went under the bridge. Alas, a potentially great acting career was nipped in the bud by a tragic accident...

CARING RAILWAY

Australians are rightly renowned throughout the world for their no-nonsense approach to life, which they combine with a robust sense of humour and a refreshing lack of sentimentality. All of these qualities were demonstrated recently when paramedics were called to remove the body of a young woman who had committed suicide by throwing herself under a train. Rather than risk getting run over themselves, they called railway officials and asked them to suspend services while they removed the body. "What's the point?" came the response from the railway company. "She's not going anywhere and this is the middle of the rush hour."

LAST SUPPER

There was a terrible aroma of "I told you so" in the air after 36-year-old Jack Boyer, a recent inmate at the Louisiana Correctional Facility, decided to celebrate his release by going to a well-known fish restaurant in New Orleans with a group of friends. After drinking a little too much for a man newly out of prison, Mr Boyer decided to complain about the fish he had been served. When asked what was wrong with the fish, he replied "It's not fresh enough. It should have come straight from the tank." Then he spied a 6-inch-long fish in the tropical display tank by his table and said "…like that". At which point he grabbed the live fish and held it in front of his mouth. Despite cries of "don't do it" Boyer dropped the fish into his mouth and attempted to swallow it whole. However, the fish was a natural born fighter. In the ensuing struggle, the fish died but managed to take Mr Boyer with him. Cause of death? Choking on a fish.

FATAL MISCALCULATION

In a story that could have come straight from a Gary Larson cartoon, a young man from Gary, Indiana died as the result of an accident during a demonstration of how to carry out bungee jumps safely. The young man, 22-year-old Jason Mason, was described by family, friends and his former teachers as a person of remarkable intelligence, and was believed to have achieved one of the highest ever IQ ratings in his home state. Their testimony makes the cause of the accident all the more surprising. Apparently the bright fellow was using a 100-foot cord to make a 50-foot bungee jump.

HARD FACED

Insurance companies often have two faces. There is the reassuring face which is so often seen in the adverts – the one that says "Trust me, like your doctor I am here to help in times of crisis" – and there is the face that appears when you have to make a claim. Anyone who doubts the validity of this description need only look to a recent court case in London, England where a former insurance broker was awarded £60,000 for the loss of his business after a car crash in which he suffered head injuries. He claimed that his business failed because the injuries had left him with a very different personality. He was now a kinder, more considerate man and, he was able to prove in court that this made him entirely unsuited to the job of an insurance broker.

CLOSE TO THE EDGE

There is nothing funny about suicide, but there are some people who fail to commit suicide in ways that are just too funny to be tragic. One such case which illustrates the point beautifully, is that of a young man who decided to stage a very public suicide by jumping from the roof of a 100-foot-high building. Fearing that his nerve might fail at the last moment, he dragged a very heavy industrial floor polisher all the way up the stairs to the top of the building. He planned to tie its power cable around his neck and shove the polisher off the building so that it would drag him over the edge. Having gone to the trouble of announcing his intentions to the crowd that had gathered outside the building, he pushed the floor polisher off the roof and waited for the cable to snap tight and drag him over. Standing there with his eyes closed he looked back over his short life and the many humiliations it had brought him. While deep in thought he heard a crash and realised that life had brought him one more. Being an industrial floor polisher, the device was fitted with a 150 feet of cable.

IF ONLY YOU HAD LISTENED...

The words "I told you so!" are arguably among the most annoying in any language. There are times, however, when their use is justified, especially in the case of a young army recruit who was stabbed to death by a friend, after he determined to prove the strength of the flak jacket he was wearing by getting his friend to stab him while wearing it. Another equally tragic tale concerns a young man who was cut down in his prime after he won a bet with a friend who said that he did not have the nerve to stick a loaded gun in his mouth and pull the trigger.

SAFETY FIRST

Some people just ask for trouble. A man in Australia found himself in hospital after setting out to repair the roof of his house – even though he took the precaution of finding a rope to tie himself to the roof. Having climbed up, he found that there was nothing to which he could attach the rope. Looking around, he noticed that his jeep, which was on the opposite side of the house, would provide a good anchor point for his rope. He climbed back down, attached the rope to the jeep's axle, threw it over the roof of his house and climbed up the other side. He tied himself firmly to the rope and set about his repairs. All went well until this wife came out of the house, jumped into the jeep and drove off.

RECORD BREAKER

An engineering firm that was quite rightly proud of its perfect safety record, decided that the best means of keeping things that way was to show its employees a film about the importance of using safety goggles while working lathes and other similar machines. Unfortunately, the film makers had been a little over enthusiastic in their desire to show just how horrific accidents involving industrial machinery and human eyes can be. The scenes caused a rapid outpouring of workers from the viewing room. As a result of the hasty exit, 25 suffered minor injuries in the crush, 13 fainted at the sight of so much blood and one man required 12 stitches to a head wound caused by striking the chair in front on his way to the floor.

A PAIN IN THE BACKSIDE

Why anyone would wish to take a hand gun to a family birthday party is a mystery but, for whatever reasons, a 21-year-old man took such a weapon to his cousin's thirtieth birthday party. He tucked it in the waistband of his trousers, gangster style, for safe keeping but, unfortunately, he left the safety catch off. The result was that he ended up shooting himself in the groin during a particularly vigorous round of pass-the-parcel. His family leapt to his aid, and his cousin, wanting to put the gun somewhere safe, removed it from the injured man's waistband and tucked it into the back of his own. As the ambulance arrived to take the casualty away to hospital the cousin reached to remove the gun from his waistband only to discover first-hand that the safety catch really was off. He shot himself in the buttocks and joined his relative in the ambulance.

A LOAD OF OLD RUBBISH

In November last year the chief of police in the city of New Haven, Connecticut, was given the unenviable task of accounting for what had happened to $23,000, which had gone missing from the police evidence room – the money had been seized during a raid on an illegal gambling den. While maintaining a straight face throughout, he explained to the sceptical press that the money must have accidentally fallen into a waste-paper basket and been thrown out with the rubbish.

LEGLESS

A woman was arrested and charged with attempted murder after trying to kill her one-legged boyfriend with a greased floor. The woman, Miss Beatrice Smithers, was picked up by the police after her neighbour, Miss Victoria Adams, reported a drunken conversation the two women had had a few days prior to the accident suffered by Miss Smithers' boyfriend. Apparently Miss Smithers had planned for some time to kill her boyfriend but had been unable to think of a way to do it without getting caught. While under the influence of alcohol, Miss Adams had suggested, jokingly, that greasing the wooden flooring at the top of the couple's staircase might result in a fatal fall down the stairs for the boyfriend. A few days later just such a fall occurred and, although it was not fatal, the police felt that they had enough evidence to bring a prosecution against Miss Smithers.

TRUE, BUT NOT SMART

A major financial institution recently gave the world an object lesson in how not to win friends and influence people. In an attempt to persuade its 2,000 richest customers to invest in a new scheme, the company carried out a mailshot which gave details of how they might become richer still by investing in extra services. As part of a trial run of the mailshot, a hapless programmer decided to create an imaginary customer called "Rich Bastard". Unfortunately, he forgot to remove this customer's name from the program and so 2,000 letters went out inviting "Dear Mr Rich Bastard" to seize a once-in-a-lifetime opportunity.

SUCKED TO DEATH

Many children stick their fingers and other things where they shouldn't, and some of them, particularly boys, carry the habit into later life. A man in New Jersey made the headlines recently when he decided to experiment by putting his penis down the pipe of his vacuum cleaner. All went well until he decided to take it just that little bit too far and switch the thing on. He had just enough time to wish he hadn't thrown the switch before a dust-sweeping blade sliced his penis off in a single swipe. The man fainted on the spot and was found in this position by his mother, who tried to tell police that he had been assaulted by a knife-wielding burglar.

HEAD FIRST

Some people never quite grow out of games of dare. Five US marines are serving prison terms after the death of a fellow marine during a game of dare that went horribly wrong. These guys were not content to play with traffic or bang on the door of a notoriously savage neighbour, they decided to take turns holding each other out of a third-floor window – by the ankles, of course. All went well until somebody dropped the ball, or rather in this case, dropped a marine.

ANIMALS

In Ireland they have a wonderful expression, only used occasionally, to describe those people who can truly be said to have a gift for comedy: "Your man could make a cat laugh". I think that must be the finest and highest compliment anyone could be paid. Cats, on the whole, do not laugh. They've been known to grin and, of course, to purr, but seldom ever has a living soul heard even so much as a snigger from any member of the feline family. And therein lies the appeal of amusing stories involving animals. Anyone who has ever become attached to a pet knows how quickly one can begin to think of it in purely human terms. We look for evidence of a growing affection between the animal and ourselves and begin to interpret its moods and behaviour as we would that of anyone else we know. Before too long we come to believe that they have a sense of humour – even if they never quite get the joke. As such, animals will always be the innocents in any comic story, a factor which makes us applaud their triumphs and giggle affectionately at their failures.

THE DOG'S BOLLOCKS

Kathy McDonie would describe her two-year-old Rottweiler Max as "...a very beautiful dog and very proud" which is partly why he became one of the first dogs in the US to receive cosmetic testicular implants. Called neuticles, the implants are designed to give the dog a fully-functional appearance. When asked why she was having her dog enhanced in this way, Mrs McDonie replied: "We want him to have his beautiful bearings". A rumour that the dog is to receive collagen lip-implants has so far proved unfounded.

TEENAGE NINJA PARROT?

Spare a thought for the poor pet shop owner in San Francisco who is facing an enormous lawsuit after a customer was attacked by a parrot. The customer, a man with his hair arranged in a ponytail, was in the bird section of the shop when the parrot took an interest in his hair. As the man walked past the bird, it jumped on to his shoulder and then lunged for his ponytail, attempting to pull it off the man's head. Mr Ponytail is currently suing for medical damages, claiming that he received a whiplash injury in the attack.

BOUND AND WAGGED

The dangers of trying to do too many things at once was illustrated by the tale of a bizarre and tragic double death that occurred in Michigan. A 79-year-old woman decided to exercise her dog and mow the lawn at the same time. In true slapstick style, the woman tied her dog to the mower and proceeded to cut the grass around her garden pond. The dog very quickly became bored and decided to make a break for it. In doing so, dog, lead, mower, and old lady became one in a tangled mass before tumbling into the pond. The dog and the old lady drowned in about six inches of water, but the mower survived with only superficial rusting.

COUCH BANANAS?

Further proof, were it needed, that we are descended from apes was provided by Twycross Zoo, in England, which is to spend nearly a quarter of a million pounds on a new play area for its gorillas. One of the most important additions to the area will be a wide-screen colour television. Apparently the gorillas love to watch TV all day, and shout and scream when it is turned off. If Charles Darwin were still around, this would surely provide him with conclusive proof of the validity of his theories on the origins of the human race.

CHICKENING OUT

A woman in New Zealand had the fright of her life recently when her dinner rose from its fiery grave and proceeded to screech at her. She was chatting with a friend when they heard a squawking chicken, apparently in some distress. They stepped outside to see who might be inflicting such extraordinary pain on the bird but could see no evidence of any such activity. Moving back into the kitchen, they discovered that the source of the noise was actually the woman's oven, in particular, the chicken that was cooking in it. Horrified, the woman tore open the oven door to find that steam was coming from the chicken's neck. This had passed through the bird's still-intact vocal chords, causing it to scream. The woman and her friend decided to settle for cheese sandwiches.

COMPLETELY BARKING

In an effort to make the lot of the far-from-average pet owner that little bit easier, a company in Illinois has come up with a novel idea – the pet-free leash (for imaginary pets). The leash, which looks like a thick length of cord, has a core of strong wire that can be adjusted to suit the size and shape of the desired imaginary pet. The handle contains a hidden switch, a battery and a pet-sound synthesizer, while the collar contains a concealed loudspeaker (presumably a woofer). The pet-sound synthesizer is capable of reproducing a variety of different barks, meows and panting noises and requires only the imagination of the pet owner to take the sonic place of a fully-formed pet. On a sinister note, however, were there ever to be a welfare service for these imaginary animals, based on the existing one, it would have the acronym RSPCIA.

IT'S THE DRINK TALKING...

A sanctuary has been set up in the West of England for the treatment of alcoholic donkeys. The sanctuary is run by Dr Elisabeth Svendsen, who explained that there was a need for the sanctuary because careless owners had been teaching their donkeys to down pints of beer but not keeping a close enough eye on their drinking habits. She explained that, while donkeys are generally placid creatures, they are more likely than humans to become addicted to alcohol and can get aggressive when they become intoxicated. She cited the case of a donkey belonging to a pub landlord that learned to down pints of beer in a single gulp. After one marathon session, it had attacked the landlord's wife because she had refused to serve it any more beer on the grounds that it was after permitted hours.

ONCE BITTEN

In a splendid variation on the "man bites dog" theme, a truly dumb animal (human in this case) decided to capture a rattlesnake he had seen cross his path. The man climbed off the bicycle he had been riding at the time, grabbed the snake in one hand and attempted to ride off. The snake was having none of this, and so bit the man on the hand. Our hero was not to be deterred and pedalled to his friend's house to show him what he had found. Once there, he produced the snake, which then bit them both. Deciding to teach the snake a lesson, the man attempted to bite it back, aiming to remove its head with a single chomp. Alas, his aim was not true – the snake was able to bite him twice more, once on the lip and once on the tongue, which resulted in a prompt visit to hospital. When asked to justify his actions, all the snake charmer could find to say in his defence was that he did it "because the snake bit me first".

BEAN AND GONE

Coffee snobs the world over are making tracks for a coffee shop in San Mateo, California, which has recently begun to stock what it calls Green Beans coffee. The coffee is not dissimilar to that made from ordinary coffee beans, with the single exception that the beans are somewhat secondhand. A large, rodent-like creature is known to feast on the beans, but like bad children everywhere, does not bother to chew before swallowing. As a result, the beans pass through its body and are excreted intact. The beans are then gathered up, roasted, ground and used to make coffee for those who can afford it. The coffee costs over $100 a pound and is available by mail order. At that price, it is probably best to save it for very special guests.

MONKEYING AROUND

Sometimes, no matter how cruel the circumstances, it can be difficult to suppress a smile when hearing a story involving animals. One such tale is that of a hunter in Uganda who is himself being hunted – by the authorities. This hunter pursues gorillas but does not kill them for food or trophies – in fact he doesn't kill them at all. This strange individual tranquillizes the gorillas, dresses them up in clown outfits and makes his getaway, leaving the gorillas to wander around looking like very hairy versions of Ronald McDonald. So far he has left six gorillas in this state, and he is roundly condemned as being especially cruel by the authorities, who have to tranquillize the gorillas and catch them a second time in order to remove the clown outfits.

FOUR-LEGGED FIEND

If ever there was a misnamed animal, at least as far as the owners are concerned, it has to be a German shepherd guide-dog who goes by the name of Lucky. This seeing-eye dog has been responsible for seeing off four of its owners, and is about to be given the opportunity to go for a fifth. The first owner died after Lucky led him out in front of a bus. The second owner was taken for a walk off the end of a pier, and the third owner was pushed under the Cologne to Frankfurt express train when the animal leapt up at him in a gesture of affection. Lucky led his fourth owner out into heavy traffic and abandoned him there to be run over by a truck. When the dog's trainer was asked if the fifth owner would be informed of Lucky's four-out-of-four record, he replied. "No. It would make the owner nervous, and Lucky nervous – and when Lucky gets nervous he's liable to do something silly."

MINAH OFFENCE

A man in Spain was up before the court charged with the attempted murder of his wife. The wife managed to convince the police that her husband was out to kill her by driving her to commit suicide. She claimed that he had trained their pet talking bird to repeat phrases such as "End it all" and "Life is not worth living". The court was not convinced by her story until she produced the bird, whereupon it proceeded to do its best raven-of-doom routine. The court found her husband guilty as charged but could not bring itself to jail the bird on the understandable grounds that it was a minah and could not, therefore, be held accountable for its actions.

BETTER THAN VIAGRA?

Anyone who has ever bought what they thought were a female pair of gerbils, mice, hamsters or guinea pigs will be well aware of the dangers of getting the sex of either of the pair wrong. Even pet shop owners, it seems, are unable to tell male and female rodents apart. This being the case, they may care to look at developments in the insect world, and in particular a new device created by an Australian research team called the "Phalloblaster". Costing around $3,500, this device is currently being used to inflate the genitalia of dead insects in order to make it easier to classify them (as male or female).

RECLUSIVE REPTILE

A pet iguana that was kept in a biology classroom in Washington, USA decided to turn the tables on its captors. Although the reptile was very well cared for, it did not welcome the attention, or even the presence, of dozens of inquisitive school children. It had noticed that whenever the alarm bell rang during the school's frequent fire drills all the children and their teacher marched out of the room, leaving the iguana to get on with important matters such as impersonating a rock. There were quite a number of false alarms before someone noticed that the iguana was always on the loose whenever they occurred. Sure enough, a little close observation revealed that the alarm was being set off deliberately by the iguana – it simply wanted to be left alone.

RATTLING GOOD FUN

There cannot be a great deal to do in Pennsylvania if activities at one local fair are anything to go by. Residents of the town of Curwensville actually pay to get into an eight-foot square cage filled with rattlesnakes. As if that wasn't foolish enough, they then attempt to pick up five of the snakes and place them in a sack in a race against the clock. The winner of this strange competition is the person who bags five snakes the fastest. As a concession to the principle, if not the practice, of safety, judges hand out time penalties to anyone who gets bitten – but only if the snake draws blood.

BOVINE BEAUTICIAN

A pedicurist in Germany has made himself a small fortune by specialising in cows. And not just any old cow can be a candidate for his attention – he restricts his service to genuine milk cows. The pedicurist, Hans Faber, charges around 100 marks per head (or 25 marks per hoof) to trim the bovines' toe nails. He also gives the hoofs a good clean. Apparently, his occupation has made him something of a minor celebrity in Germany and he is often invited to parties where people queue up to ask him about his occupation.

A LOOSE MOOSE

Many people imagine scientists to be deeply dull individuals who spend their time peering into the dark corners of the Universe and attempting to find bigger and better ways to blows us all up or put us all back together again afterwards. This is clearly not the case with conservation biologist Joel Berger of the University of Nevada. In order to get up close to a herd of moose, Dr Berger donned a disturbingly convincing moose costume during his field research. His biggest worry during these expeditions wearing the moose costume, which apparently also involved throwing wolf dung at the moose to see if it annoyed them, was being spotted by an amorous male moose...

THREE BULL CIRCUS

There was a time, during Hemingway's day, when bullfighters were considered romantic figures, brave men who would enter the arena without thought for personal safety or a trace of fear on their faces. Times, fortunately, change, as do opinions. Things have declined so much that the world's major bullfighting event ended in farce after the organisers attempted to save money from their overstretched budgets by using cheaper, and noticeably more docile, bulls. The crowd hissed and booed during the first three fights, which were abandoned after each of the bulls refused to fight. In an attempt to save the event, the organisers painted white spots on the three bulls and sent them back into the ring. All went well until the crowd noticed that the matadors' clothes were getting whiter with each pass of the bulls.

NIL BY MOUTH

Anyone who has ever tried to administer medicine to a sick pet will understand the problems involved in getting the patient to take the medication. We know it tastes bad, the animal knows it tastes bad, and the animal is sick so the last thing it wants to do at a time like this is to be is be messed around by the monkey who usually feeds it. Pity, then, the keepers of a sick elephant at San Francisco Zoo, who had refused to take its medication. Together with a local vet, they came up with a way of delivering the medicine but, as a spokesman for the zoo said, "It's not something you'd do for fun". Without going into details, it involved a 2 pound 10 inch suppository, a couple of handfuls of cocoa butter, and a team of four, increasingly unwilling, volunteers.

HAIRY STORY

One occasionally hears sad stories of creatures that gnaw off their own limbs in order to escape from traps. This scenario comes to mind when imagining being stuck in a lift with a group of farmers from Iowa who have been competing to discover who owns the world's largest cow hairball. At one time the hairball that gave rise to an enviable entry in the record books was owned by Lucian Langhorn, a farmer. One of his cows produced a hairball that was nearly 40 inches in diameter. Unfortunately for him, his prize-winning hairball has been surpassed by a cow owned by his brother. Lucian's brother, Lloyd, now lays claim to the record with a hairball that has a remarkable diameter of 45 inches.

DEATH BY PIG

A group of Russian farmhands were eating lunch one day when they were disturbed by the sound of a squealing pig coming from one of the manure pits. One of the farmhands rushed over to the pit and discovered a pig thrashing around inside it. He climbed down ten feet or so into the pit, only to be overcome by the powerful methane fumes inside. Seeing that he had collapsed, his friend jumped in to save him, but he also collapsed. The one remaining farmhand, alarmed that his friends were in serious trouble, leapt in after them, only to suffer the same fate. All three men died, but the pig lived to squeal another day.

NOT DEAD, JUST RESTING...

This near-legendary story concerns the tale of a crew member involved in the America's Cup yacht race who accidentally ran over a kangaroo while sightseeing in the outback in Australia. The sailor decided to prop the dead kangaroo up against the side of the car, put his blazer on the poor creature, and take a picture of the resulting image. All went well until the kangaroo, which had only been stunned, woke up, realized that all was not well and made a break for it, taking the blazer, three credit cards, one passport and $1,000 in cash.

HOT STUFF

Three men from Singapore decided to "punish" a hungry rat they found eating their lunches. One of the men managed to capture the rat and another poured paint thinner over it. Unfortunately for the three men, the friend with the paint thinner was more than a little clumsy and so they all ended up cover in the stuff. This was not a problem until the third man decided to set fire to the rat...himself and his two colleagues. One of the men died as a result of severe burns and another was sentenced to five months in prison.

HOLE IN ONE

A golfer in Wales approached the last hole of the course, which he opened with a magnificent driving shot, which astonished not only himself and his golfing partner, but also a passing sheep. The hapless creature had the bad luck to be positioned in such a way that the ball flew straight up its behind. Such was the poor creature's shock and surprise at what happened that it raced off, carrying the golfer's ball with it. The golfer assumed that he was going to have to concede the hole, so imagine his surprise when the sheep, still running, ran across the course, on to the green and deposited the ball by the Eighteenth Hole.

PENGUIN PUSHOVER

Bored Royal Air Force pilots in the Falklands Islands took to keeping themselves amused by playing games with the local penguin population. The birds appeared to be fascinated by the low-flying jets and often resembled spectators at a tennis match, their heads going back and forth as the aeroplanes passed by. The game involved the pilots first making a pass from left to right to catch the birds' attention before flying from right to left to make sure that they all penguin eyes were on the planes. Then it was time to make a final pass from left to right. Up to 10,000 penguins at a time have been known to tumble backwards as they attempted to follow the jets passing overhead.

SNAKES ALIVE

A father and his young daughter were visiting a fairground when they noticed a merry-go-round. It was of the classic variety, with ornately painted wooden horses which went up and down on poles. "Can I have a go Daddy?" asked the young girl, and in no time at all found herself going round and round on the rather shabby old ride. After a short while she called out to her father. "The horsie is biting me" she cried. "Don't be silly, dear," her father replied, "those horses don't bite." As the ride came to an end the father stepped forward to lift his daughter off the ride, only to discover that the horses really were biting – or at least the snakes that they were riddled with were.

CONFUSED CANINE

A police dog in Canada was dismissed from the force after just one year in service. The dog seemed to have decided that it would choose its own friends and not have the choice imposed on him by the police. This would not normally cause a problem with most dogs, but having trained the animal to attack on command, the police found that they had difficulties controlling just whom the confused animal attacked. In a number of different situations, the dog, on receiving the attack command, would look at his handler, look at the villain and then make his own choice. Unfortunately this meant that the dog sometimes attacked his handler, holding the officer in place while the villains made their escape.

MANCUBS

Four-year-old Berci Kutrovics was discovered wandering around western Hungary walking on all fours and behaving like a dog. When the authorities looked into the matter, they found that the boy had been neglected by his parents to such an extent that he had ended up being reared by the family dogs. This meant that the boy sniffed his food before eating and slept curled up with the pets. Even more remarkable was the case of a 12-year-old boy, discovered in the Sri Lankan jungle in 1973, who had been raised by monkeys. He was able to communicate with his "parents" by means of grunts and yelps and could be relied upon to swing through the trees with the best of the apes.

BOVINE DEODORANT

During the Cold War the US Army got up to some very silly things. Top of the list of these has to be the story which has recently come to light as a result of the Freedom Of Information Act. In the early Sixties, a crack team of Uncle Sam's finest special forces troops staged daring raids on cattle stockyards in six cities across the country. Armed only with cans of deodorant, the Green Berets entered the yards in the dead of night and used the aerosols to spray as many of the unsuspecting cows as they could find. In a later report, it was revealed that the purpose of their mission was to demonstrate how easy it would have been for the communist foe to enter a stockyard and spread deadly viruses in the same way.

BEATEN BY BEES

Two neighbours in Sale, a suburb of Manchester, England decided between them that the best way to rid themselves of a bees' nest that had appeared near their houses was to blow the thing up. Armed with a Second World War hand grenade and after drinking too many pints of beer, the men – known only as Dave and Pete – crept up to the hive, placed the grenade underneath, pulled the pin and ran…but not far enough. The resulting explosion peppered both men with a small amount of shrapnel, shattered 16 windows and set off car alarms for miles around. Deciding that they needed hospital treatment, the two men headed for their cars, only to be met by a swarm of very angry bees. It was at this point that one of the men discovered that he was severely allergic to the venom and as a result spent 14 days in intensive care. Neither man has retained a taste for honey.

POISONOUS PASTILLES

A woman in Alabama tried to convince a jury that her husband's death was an accident. The woman, who reputedly enjoyed a very stormy relationship with her deceased spouse, claimed that he died as a result of a practical joke, initiated by him, which went horribly wrong. Apparently he had decided to play a joke on his wife by taking a small poisonous snake and hiding it in a large bag of sweets before handing them to her. She took the sweets and was about to reach into it when she felt the snake moving in the bag. In a blind panic, she dropped the packet and the snake shot out, slithered across the floor and proceeded to make its way up her husband's trouser leg. Fearing for her husband's life, the wife reached for a shotgun and attempted to shoot the snake. Unfortunately she aimed too high and ended up blowing her husband's head off while the snake made its getaway.

COWABUNGA

In the United Kingdom it is against the law to allow a dangerous wild animal to roam free where it might harm people. One animal that is not covered by the act, however, is the humble cow. This four-legged beast has not been deemed to be a danger to humans but the government may have to think again after a recent story in *The Times* was brought to the attention of its Health And Safety Executive. An elderly woman and her four dogs were found trampled to death in a field in Sussex and all the evidence points to death by cow. Police, investigating the matter, issued a dangerous cows warning to all would-be ramblers.

PIGGED OUT

Fate can be awfully cruel, especially, it seems, to those who are just trying to do a good turn. Take, for example, the story of two animal-rights protesters in Germany, who took it upon themselves to free several thousand pigs who were to be slaughtered the following day. With commando-like skill, the activists scaled the perimeter fence of the slaughter house, avoided detection on the closed-circuit cameras and managed to make their way along a narrow passageway to where the animals were being stored prior to slaughter. Armed with bolt cutters, they removed the padlock that secured the gate of the animal enclosure but, unfortunately, greatly alarmed the animals in the process. Before either of them had time to contemplate the problems this might cause, several thousands pigs made a break for freedom up the narrow passageway along which the animal rights activists had just crept. Their crushed bodies were found by police who arrived to investigate what the commotion was about.

BARKING MAD

In the United States an insurance company came under fire for refusing to insure any more dogs of the much-maligned pit bull breed. Things reached such a point that the leader of the Pit Bull Owner's Association went on record to state that the behaviour of the insurance company amounted to little more than "Dog racism".

101 ALSATIONS (ALMOST)

Dog lovers will be moved by the plight of an elderly man in New Jersey who was ordered by a judge to do something about his dogs. Neighbours took out a joint action against him claiming, among other things, that his dogs were tormenting them at nights with their incessant howling and general pack-like behaviour. The situation reached a head when police arrived to request that he do something about the noise only to discover that he was keeping not three or four dogs at the house – as first supposed – but over 60. The dogs, all Alsations, were discovered to be both healthy and happy, which caused problems for the neighbours whose legal action hinged on the dogs being maltreated. Then some bright spark came up with a novel idea. The poor man was forced to get rid of his dogs on the grounds that he was, in effect, running an unlicensed "kennel" and was not fit to do so on the grounds of his addiction – to dogs.

PILLOW FRIGHT

Snakes seem to figure largely in bizarre stories, probably because most of use would prefer not to encounter them in domestic situations. One person who had a first-class opportunity to appreciate the thrill of meeting a snake unexpectedly in her home is Beverley Sharpe, who was living in a small town on the border between Holland and Germany. She was woken in the night by the sensation that something was pressing down on her pillow. At first she ignored it, believing that she had imagined the sensation. When it persisted, however, she felt compelled to switch on her bedside light and investigate – and there on her pillow was a six-foot-long boa constrictor. The snake, called "Feathers", had escaped from a neighbour's house several weeks earlier and was trying to find its way back.

MONKEY MAN

He walks upright, enjoys a nice cup of coffee in the morning and is rather partial to a drop of brandy before bedtime. Oliver the ape, the latest creature to be causing a controversy at the zoo where he is being kept, was born in 1969, and is not like other apes. He has a smaller head than most, the top half of his body is hairless, and he has a square jaw. Like many humans, he enjoys watching television. He even knows how to use – and flush – a toilet. Oliver is not happy, however, in the company of other apes as they shun him because he is so different from them. So different, in fact, that some people have alleged that he is a chimpanzee-human hybrid, the product of a bizarre and unethical experiment. While it is hard to imagine scientists ever behaving in this way, there is no getting over the fact that a large amount of Oliver's leisure time is spent pursuing his keeper's wife.

PARTYING PACHYDERMS

The authorities in the Indian state of Assam have been forced to turn to professional hunters in an effort to do something about a rather unique problem that has been plaguing the state: drunken, rampaging elephants. This drastic action was taken after the latest outrage, which resulted in the deaths of 13 people and injuries to nearly 20 more. The problem arose after the practice of homebrewing became increasingly popular in remote villages. The elephants were able to drink some of the left overs from this process and soon acquired quite a taste for it. It is believed that the latest incident was sparked after the elephants caught a whiff of homebrew and went in search of its source. Unable to get into the houses where it was being made, the elephants simply tried to barge their way in, killing and injuring as they went.

RAT'S REVENGE

When a 400-year-old thatched cottage burnt down in the village of Puddledock in Norfolk, England residents were at a loss to explain how it had happened. The cottage was empty at the time of the fire and was set well back from the road, away from any stray sparks or any other sources of heat. The most popular theory among the villagers was that the fire must have been caused by a bird which picked up a discarded cigarette while it was still burning and then dropped it on to the roof. The truth, however, turned out to be even stranger than fiction. Accident investigators, working on behalf of an insurance company, were able to discover that the fire had been started by a rat. Apparently the rat had eaten a phosphor-based poison before climbing into the roof space to die. As its body decomposed, the poison was broken down into pure phosphor, which burst into flames when maggots, chewing on the rat, exposed it to the air.

FROZEN FISHERMEN

Ice fishing is a sport that has become very popular in Russia over the last decade. It involves squatting in sub-zero temperatures over holes cut in the ice of a frozen lake. The water below the ice is black because of the covering of ice and it is very rare indeed for fish to actually come anywhere near the holes. The many Russians who indulge in the sport claim that it is the ultimate in relaxation techniques even though around 100 anglers a year die as a result of exposure or drowning.

CAT CRAZY

At a time when the whole Russian economy is in a state of flux, when rich Russians choose to pay taxes to the Mafia rather than the State and where many ordinary Russian citizens cannot be certain that they will have food in a week's time, one enterprise is thriving. I refer, of course, to the Cat Theatre of Moscow, a 300-seater venue that is sold out months in advance. The theatre's founder and chief cat trainer, Yuri Kuklachev, has succeeded where millions of blue-rinsed old ladies have failed, having trained the cats to walk tightropes, push trains and play leap frog.

PIG PARTY

No one would have thought it, but it seems that pigs are party animals. Not content with being the source of all manner of breakfast goodies, the pig can also be relied upon to keep on boogying until after midnight. Or at least that's what researchers at an agricultural centre near Reading would have us believe. Not content with using the animal for food, the researchers have taken to spying on the pigs in their care and, after months of careful study, are able to report back that the average pig likes nothing better than to eat, drink and make merry when the farmer isn't looking.

DO BEARS STEAL IN THE WOODS?

Staff at the Yosemite National Park have had to deal with a huge increase in the number of complaints about break-ins to cars left unattended in the park. In one month alone, there were 600 break-ins and the problem appeared to be getting well and truly out of hand. Despite constant requests not to leave their cars unattended with tempting items on display, visitors to the park continued to take little notice – and continued to return to cars that had been broke into and often left in a real mess. The culprits are well-known to the park employees but they have been unable to do anything about the thefts, which are mostly of food items. Said Steve Thompson, who is a wildlife biologist at the park: "My problem starts when the smarter bears and the dumber visitors intersect."

MANURE MOUNTAINS

It seems that even animals are not safe from the attentions of the United States Environmental Protection Agency. In a new move, the agency is seeking to limit the amount of pollution produced by livestock farms after it was revealed that farm animals in the US produce, on average, 30 times more manure than the average US citizen. In support of the new legislation, the agency points out that one farm currently under construction in the state of Utah will, when finished, be responsible for producing more "manure" than all the citizens of the city of Los Angeles can produce in a comparable amount of time.

LAP OF LUXURY

The news that a sanctuary for stray animals has been erected in the city of Pasadena at a cost estimated to be in the region of four million reinforces the view that Californians really are determined attention seekers. The sanctuary is equipped with luxury cages, an aviary, a garden and a staff of animal counsellors who are more than willing to talk over any problems the pampered creatures in their care might be having. A similar centre was opened in San Francisco but, in an effort to avoid any unfavourable criticism, the management of the centre promised to allow a few homeless people into the building for the occasional night in order to provide companionship for any animals who become lonely of an evening.

CAT CONUNDRUM

Two houses in Palmers Green, North London, were recently condemned as health hazards after their owners allowed cats on to the premises. All went well at first but matters got out of hand when the felines began to mate. Before too long one of the houses became home to 32 cats while the neighbouring house became home to an incredible 54 cats. The houses came to the attention of the authorities after neighbours complained to the local council about the smell and the noise at night. It is a pity that the council couldn't afford to deport the cats to Vietnam. That unfortunate country is still suffering a severe shortage of cats after they became a fashionable food item. As a result, the country is over-run with rats.

WEIGHTS AND MEASURES

In Florida they are very strict on their laws, rules and regulations regarding the keeping of domestic pets. There are rules regarding the maximum number of pets any resident of the former swamp land can keep – basically, you're allowed four pets unless, of course, one of them is a fish, and then you're allowed to have five pets. You can actually have five pets (excluding fish) so long as they are all under ten pounds in weight. Ten pets are permissible, however, if none of them is over one pound in weight and, under certain conditions, you can have up to 25 pets, but only so long as they are all fish.

PENGUIN PROSTITUTES

A researcher from the University of Cambridge who had been studying the mating habits of penguins for five years, made a surprising discovery in the course of her investigations. While observing the female penguins, she noticed that many of them were willing to trade sex in return for nest-building stones from males who were not their established partners. In almost all cases, the sex took place when the usual mate wasn't looking. The researcher, Dr Fiona Hunter, also observed that the male "clients" tended to leave a few extra stones after the act had taken place, as if to "tip" the female for service rendered. This is, she believes, the first recorded instance of prostitution by non-humans.

CRIME

It is inevitable that crime should be the longest section in this book because it is in the area of criminal activity that you find the most bizarre behaviour. The reason for this is simple: even assuming that the law is an ass, it does act as a filter. We all know the consequences of getting caught while committing a criminal act and so most of us choose not to break the law in any significant way. This leaves behind those who have little choice but to break the law, and those who break the law believing that they will never be caught. In short, this section deals with the desperate and the deluded. These people drove a lawyer friend of mine to abandon criminal law because he was so depressed by the sheer stupidity of those he was called upon to represent. Some of his cases would have made a valuable addition to this book, but demonstrated levels of delusion and foolishness that were simply beyond belief. Instead, I shall present to you tales of criminals who could be deemed, by their behaviour, to be merely insane.

NUTTY KILLER

We've all heard stories of people who attempt to kill their partners with knives or guns, but members of the jury in a trial in Montreal, Canada, were more than a little surprised to find themselves listening to a case of a woman accused of trying to murder her husband with a handful of peanut butter. The 29-year-old woman was arrested and charged with attempted murder after she spread peanut butter over her husband's face while he slept, knowing that he had a severe allergy to nuts. The poor man only survived because a choking fit woke him up just in time for him to inject himself with an antidote.

PINK PANTHER?

After receiving reports that a bank robber had fled to a shopping mall in Los Angeles, police rushed to the scene and began to search for a likely-looking suspect. The task proved not to be too difficult – the description of the robber indicated that they were looking for a man in his thirties, carrying a briefcase and wearing a plain grey business suit and not-so-matching pink slippers. When arrested, the man could offer no reason as to why he was wearing the slippers. A spokesman for the LAPD made the following statement: "The suit worked very well for him, but he should have realized that the pink slippers were simply too radical a fashion statement".

BOVINE AVIATION

The crew of a Japanese trawler was rescued from the Sea of Japan recently, only to be arrested within a few moments of setting foot on land. The fact that their boat had sunk was not the cause for arrest, but the excuse they gave was. They claimed that they had been sailing in calm waters when a cow fell from the sky, crashed through the boat and caused it to sink in under a minute. They were later released when the crew of a Russian freight plane came forward and confessed to having thrown a stolen cow out of their aeroplane at 30,000 feet because the cow had broken loose of its restraints and started to cause havoc on board the plane. Rather than risk further damage to the aircraft, they had ejected the cow into the open sea below, assuming that no one would be any the wiser.

BATTLING GRANDMA

At least one bank robber is going to think twice before threatening any more middle-aged Spanish women during a robbery. The robber was attempting to hold up a bank in Madrid, Spain when a woman seized the opportunity to knock the gun out of his hands, throw him to the ground and administer a good kicking. The man had burst into the bank armed with a toy gun and with some fake explosives strapped to his body. The woman was so offended that he should try to hold her up with such obvious fakes that she was driven to extreme violence. Police are currently investigating whether or not this is the same robber who fled from the same bank a year earlier when the same woman resisted attempts to rob her and her fellow customers.

KNOTTY PROBLEM

Anyone who doubts that cartoons can kill should examine the case of Rayton Jerome Bullok, an 18-year-old prisoner at the Allegheny County Jail in Pittsburgh. Bullok fell to his death from the eighth floor of the prison block after attempting to escape by breaking a window with a chair and then lowering himself down using a rope made from bed sheets. No one had warned him that this only works in cartoons and Bullok fell 100 feet to his death as soon as he put his weight on to the knotted sheets. Reports that he had been seen earlier in the day trying to kill an animated mouse with the aid of a frying pan have so far proved unfounded

RHINESTONE RAIDER

A 17-year-old country-and-western fan is facing the unusual criminal charge of attempting to rob a bank while dressed as a cowboy. After parking his pick-up truck (which had the name 'Trigger' painted on the side) outside the bank, the boy marched up to the counter, pulled a six-gun from the holster on his belt and shouted "This is a stick up!" Far from having the desired effect, this reduced the bank staff to tears of laughter. The boy was heard to shout "Giddyup" and "Yee Haa" as he drove away from the scene of the failed raid.

BUSTED BY INVITATION

Dope smokers the world over seem to be welcoming the tendency of many police forces to turn a blind eye to what the law is beginning to see as a fairly harmless habit. However, even the police can only lighten up so much. Two officers arrived at a house in Massachusetts after someone accidentally dialled 911 and then hung up. After being invited into the house, the officers were surprised to find marijuana being smoked. They were going to let it pass until the lady of the house proudly showed them a huge store of the stuff in the kitchen. The woman and her husband were a little taken aback to find themselves in court on charges of cultivating and supplying marijuana.

CAUGHT IN CASUALTY

Proof that what goes around comes around is provided by the heartwarming tale of a doctor working the Saturday night casualty shift in a hospital in London, England. Among the usual broken heads was a victim of a stabbing. While treating the victim, the doctor recognized his patient as the man who had held him up at knife point in a London club some months earlier. Having treated the man's wound, the doctor summoned the police who promptly arrested and charged the man with nine offences, including the one against the doctor.

PROFESSIONAL CRIMINAL

In a textbook example of how not to rob a post office, a 29-year-old man in London, England forgot to wear his mask, was unable to open the post office safe and had to settle for the money in the tills. Because the money bags were so heavy, he enlisted the help of two small children, who held the post office door open for him and helped him to load the money into his car. They then walked by the side of his car as he tried to negotiate his way through the rush-hour traffic, noting his registration number before saying goodbye. The man later turned up at a hotel, where he placed the stolen money in the safe and specifically asked the receptionist not to tell the police he was there. When questioned shortly afterwards, the man denied the charges made against him, but slipped up when asked for his occupation, which he gave as "Armed Robber".

SHOP TILL YOU DROP

There can be little doubt as to the intentions of a woman who went out with a shopping list that read: chainsaw, knife, rifle, bullets… and pizza. The 35-year-old woman went home, fed the pizza to the kids and the bullets to her husband. After shooting him, she climbed into bed with the body and made an unsuccessful attempt to commit suicide using the same rifle that she had used on her husband. She faced two charges: second-degree murder, and owning a chainsaw without a permit.

UNLIKELY STORY

Anyone who has ever suffered from writer's block is unlikely to feel much sympathy for an Iranian author who was in a divorce court recently answering charges that he regularly beat his wife. He claimed in his defence that he did so in order to monitor her response and thereby be able to make a more realistic attempt to capture her hurt and pain in his writing. The judge was not fooled for a moment: the man faced a jail term unless he could convince his wife to forgive him.

CAUGHT BY THE CORTEGE

Some people are just cursed with bad luck. A robber in New Jersey was busy making his getaway when he drove into a funeral procession for a police officer who had been shot and killed in the line of duty. Rather than doing the sensible thing and slowing down, the man attempted to escape by running over the officers who were walking by the side of the coffin. The officers opened fire and the robber's car eventually came to a halt when he crashed into not one, but two police cars. The robber is unlikely to keep his licence after the incident.

DYING FOR A CIGARETTE

A man was shot and wounded when police approached him on the New York subway and demanded that he extinguish his cigarette. Standing up for the God-given right of smokers the world over to light up wherever they damn well please, the man refused and took a swing at the officers before attempting to run off. He might have got away with it had he not then produced a gun and fired at the pursuing police. He was wounded in the exchange and is currently helping the police with their inquiries.

RONALD MCDONALD THE BAD

It's official: Ronald McDonald (no relation) is a child molester. After spending 13 years working in child care and helping to teach young children at his local church, Ronald C McDonald confessed to molesting seven children in his care, although police believe he harmed many more children than this. Currently being held on two counts of child rape, Ronald McDonald will no longer be available to play Santa at children's parties and concerned parents will have to look elsewhere for an inexpensive and willing baby sitter.

ROCK 'N' ROBBIN'

A thief in Tucson learned first-hand that sticks and stones can break bones. After helping himself to a car stereo, and setting off the alarm in the process, the thief made a run for it, little realizing that the car's alarm had disturbed a neighbour of the car's owner. Rushing out to see what was going on, the neighbour picked up a rock and threw it at the robber, knocking him out and putting an end to his hopes of escape. Police praised the neighbour's prompt action but warned that throwing rocks in a situation like this can be dangerous.

FALL FROM GRACE

Many people consider themselves to be above the law, but a homeless man in Mississippi proved himself to be quite literally so when he fell through the roof of the Jackson Police Department headquarters. It emerged that he had been living there for quite some time, as seen by the accumulation of such belongings as dozens of cereal boxes, countless newspapers and magazines, and numerous copies of the Bible. The unfortunate man was arrested after his fall from grace and charged with the destruction of city property.

LOW GRADE BURGLARS

It's not just the police who are getting younger these days. Burglars broke into a house recently and stole money, a watch and a skateboard. Unfortunately, however, they left a couple of rather telling clues behind – their school books. After being picked up from school by the police, the boys admitted to the burglary and asked for 14 other offences to be taken into consideration. On the plus side, they were at least telling the truth when they told their teacher that they had lost their homework.

CONSUMER RIGHTS ACTIVIST...

In recent years we've come to expect a certain standard of attention in shops and banks, and few people are now slow in coming forward with complaints about poor service. This trend was taken to its logical conclusion by a bank robber who demanded her hand-over-the-money note back after she felt that the bank staff were taking too long to serve her. Exercising her rights as both consumer and bank robber, she made her way to the next bank up the street, where she received faster and more courteous attention.

STEALING A KISS?

Just when you thought that the average villain couldn't get any dumber, a robber in Pasadena, who had stolen a woman's purse after holding her up at gunpoint, wrote to her to tell her that he thought she was beautiful and to ask her for a date. He passed on his pager number and waited for her to get in touch, which she did. At first the robber ignored the pager, but later took to leaving messages on her answering machine. These were eventually traced to a local store and the robber was captured. He explained in court that he regretted his actions and hoped to see the woman again – when he gets out of prison.

OUT OF THE FRYING PAN...

Believing that her husband had been unfaithful, a Chinese woman decided to confront him about it, but not with strong words. Instead, she waited until he was asleep and then woke him, screamed her accusations and poured a pan of boiling fat over him. Her husband was left with serious burns to his right shoulder, scalp and ear. As soon as he had stopped screaming – which was roughly when the police arrived – he explained that she was mistaken and that he was not guilty of the charge she had levelled at him. Taking her cue from her husband, the woman denied causing grievous bodily harm with intent to kill, when faced with the charge in court.

PHONE CHARGES

A 14-year-old boy in Florida decided that it was about time his sister got off the phone. He pleaded with her, taunted her, shouted at her and threatened her, but she would not put the receiver down. Eventually, he became so incensed by the amount of time his 15-year-old sister was spending on the telephone that he fetched his father's gun and shot her. Police are now considering exactly what to charge him with, and his parents are considering getting an extra telephone line. The sister survived, but is somewhat reluctant to use the telephone.

COMING UP FOR AIR...

An Australian man has been sentenced to four-and-a-half years in prison after his partner died while performing oral sex on him in a swimming pool. Apparently the couple had already had sex in the pool in a multitude of positions when the man grabbed his partner and forced her head under water. While she initially took the hint and went along with his request, her attempts to surface for air were prevented when he became excited and held her under the water.

CAREER CHANGE

The importance of good, clear handwriting was illustrated by the case of a bank robber who found himself unable to rob banks using the tried and trusted method of handing a note to the person at the counter demanding huge sums of cash in return for not getting shot. More often than not his note was handed back by the bank teller, who would complain that his handwriting was illegible. The robber has since taken up mugging.

CHILD SECURITY

The cost of living is always rising, so much so that a woman in Detroit was forced to hand over her son to a drug dealer in order to settle a $1,000 debt she owed the man. The case came to the attention of the local police when the 15-year-old boy's grandmother discovered that he was missing. She had decided to drop in on him while his mother was in prison serving time for a totally unrelated burglary.

DEATH BEFORE FREEDOM

Observe, if you will, the cruel hand of fate at work in the case of a man who had been wrongly charged on six counts of sexually assaulting a 13-year-old boy. Throughout his trial, the man, Francis Cavaliere, aged 40, had protested his innocence and as the case progressed it became increasingly clear that he truly was innocent. As he rose to hear the verdict of the jury, he seemed visibly unwell, despite the fact that the answer "Not guilty" was read out in response to each of the charges put to the jury by the judge. As the final charge was read out, the man collapsed and died. Had he lived long enough, he would have learned that he was found not guilty on all charges.

BUTT NAKED

The owner of a popular pizza parlour in New York City was arrested by police and charged with indecent exposure after he dropped his pants outside a local school and asked pupils to initial his buttocks. The 29-year-old man, Franco Pezzuto, had approached a group of young boys and shown them naked pictures of himself before offering $30 to anyone who would sign his arse. He was later captured by police, who had been investigating a number of similar incidents. He admitted the offences but was unable to provide the police with a motive for his actions.

MONEY FOR NOTHING?

America has seen a dramatic rise in the number of nuisance lawsuits taken out by inmates of its prisons. On the surface, these may seem to be little more than a frivolous way of passing the time until release, but some of these lawsuits have been successful. For instance, prisoner Richard Burton was awarded $2,000 after he complained that the prison chilli he had been served had hurt his stomach. Prisoner Lawrence Bittaker was awarded $4,500 after complaining that, and we quote, his "cookie was broken". Most unusual of all was the case of Prisoner Kevin Howard, who was awarded $18,500 after complaining that his thoughts were being broadcast over the prison's public address system.

STICKY PREDICAMENT

There was an admirable streak of logic in the thinking of one Sergio De Sa, an addicted glue sniffer. For years he stole glue in small quantities from neighbourhood shops, but realized that if he was ever to achieve a true nirvana-like state of intoxication he would have to go and get the glue at source. One weekend he managed to break into the glue factory where his favourite product was made and proceeded to make the most of the fumes coming directly from the enormous vats that he found there. He became so overwhelmed that he collapsed onto the floor, knocking over a large quantity of glue in the process. When he eventually came round, he found that he had become stuck to the floor and was only discovered 36 hours later when staff arrived for work on Monday morning. Unfortunately, the glue factory's product was so effective that police had to cut the floor around Sergio in order to take him into custody.

HEAD CASE

During a routine house-search for marijuana, police in Los Angeles came across a box marked 'Eight-piece Party Kit'. Along with the usual assortment of bongs, rolling papers, filters and gauzes, officers found a genuine human head wrapped in a white lab coat. A collection of photographs, also found in the kit, revealed that the head had been the life and (departed?) soul of many a stoned get-together. The pictures showed that potheads all over California must have been queuing up to have their pictures taken with a real head. Some shots even showed people eating dinner while the head was sitting on the table. An autopsy revealed that the head was that of a woman. When questioned by police, its owner revealed that he had bought it from a student at a now-defunct medical school in Kansas.

NUMB NUTS

A villain demonstrated just what balls he had when he attempted to leap a tall metal fence while fleeing from the police. Although one of the officers giving chase managed to grab hold of 24-year-old Jamie Johnson's leg, he managed to kick himself free and eventually cleared the fence. Unfortunately for Jamie, he was apprehended a few streets away and taken to the local police station to be formally charged. While there, officers noticed that

Jamie's crotch was bleeding. A doctor was called and closer inspection revealed that Mr Johnson had left his testicles behind on the metal fence.

A DOG'S LUCK

In an apparently motiveless crime in Long Beach, robbers climbed out of an old grey truck, held up a 14-year-old boy at gunpoint and stole his dog. Police are puzzled as to why they might have done this, as the dog is old, infirm, and blind in one eye. When the robbery was reported, the police had assumed that the animal would be a rare breed or a prize-winning show dog, but they were forced to put the robbery down to the fact that the dog was unfortunate enough to be unarmed and living in California.

EXECUTIVE STRESS RELIEF

Executives are always harping on about the stresses and strains of their jobs, and there may be a degree of truth in what they have to say. Certainly it could be the only possible explanation for the behaviour of a 34-year-old executive in Boston who had an argument with his wife after she accused him of overcooking the pasta. Rather than stopping at a few well-chosen harsh words, the stressed-out executive ripped out his wife's heart and lungs and nailed them to a stake in a neighbour's garden. He then went and knocked on the neighbour's door and attempted to engage him in a conversation about gun control. When charged with murder, the executive entered a Not Guilty charge.

SHORT-SIGHTED VIEW

In one of the best-ever excuses offered in mitigation of multiple charges of theft, a visually-impaired employee of the US Forestry Service claimed, first, that he had come to believe that it was standard practice to, as he put it, to borrow any items belonging to the government that were considered surplus to requirements. When it was pointed out to him that he had borrowed truckloads of items his second line of defence was that, because of his visual impairment, he simply had not noticed that he still had so many items to return.

PART-TIME CRIME

The age-old adage that one should set a thief to catch a thief has been taken a little too literally by the Chicago police force. Remarkably, in a city cursed with high levels of gang-related crime, the policemen's union protects the right of police officers to be gang members outside of work time. In the last three years, 15 officers have been charged with gang-related crime, and in the latest case, a 34-year-old police officer was arrested after trying to sell two pounds of cocaine to undercover colleagues.

PASS THE PROZAC

Ronald M Chroniak, 46, decided to spread a little happiness one Friday afternoon – so he walked into the Las Vegas branch of Bank Of America, politely robbed it of a large sum of cash and then strolled outside handing out $100 bills to passers-by, requesting nothing in return other than that they "Have a nice day". When he handed one of the notes to a man who was eating lunch in the bank's courtyard, he was asked where he'd got the money from. The robber smiled and replied, "I just robbed the bank. Have a nice day."

DEAF AND STUPID

The words "white supremacist" and "intellectual giant" are rarely heard in the same sentence, but Donald Leroy Evans surprised even case-hardened court officials with the level of his ignorance. On trial for the murder of a prostitute in Fort Lauderdale, Evans applied to court to be allowed to wear his Ku Klux Klan robes and be addressed in court as "Hi Hitler". He also requested that his name be changed in all court documents to "the honourable and respected name of Hi Hitler". Court officials were initially puzzled by his request, until they realized that Evans was under the mistaken impression that the followers of Adolf Hitler had said "Hi Hitler" rather than "Heil Hitler".

MUSICAL ESCAPE

Objections to the idea of staging classical opera in modern costumes have been many and varied, but an incident in Birmingham, England, provided another possible reason for sticking to traditional costume. For reasons known only to themselves, a City of Birmingham Opera company had elected to perform Figaro dressed as members of the far-right (but very wrong) National Front. All went well until one of the luvvies stepped outside to make a phone call and was confronted by two black men who were not at all impressed by his Union Jack shirt and radical haircut. They ignored his claim that he was simply a baritone going about his business and were about to give him a severe beating when he burst into an aria. Clearly this is more than even the toughest of hardmen can take and so they fled, leaving the singer to make his call.

HOLY DROPPINGS, BATPEOPLE

In Thailand, bat dung is quite a valuable commodity. The quest for bat dung led to tragedy recently for one team of dung collectors as they came out of a bat cave to the North-East of the country's capital, Bangkok. A rival gang of dung prospectors (gangsters or dungsters, maybe?) tossed a grenade into their path. Five men were killed and two were seriously injured. The report did not mention whether or not any of the bats suffered in the incident.

YOU AGAIN?

Bank robbers do not come much dumber than the man who walked into a branch of the Bank Of Montreal claiming to have a gun hidden under his coat and demanding $2,000 in cash. Staff handed him the money and he was able to make his escape before the police arrived. He might just have got away with his crime had he not returned later in the day, this time without his coat, and attempted to open an account. Although he looked familiar, staff had some doubts that this new customer was the man who had robbed the bank earlier in the day. However, these doubts were soon dispelled when he was asked just how much he would like to deposit. "Oh, $2,000 – in cash," he boasted.

JUST LIKE ARNIE

A man in Florida had his wallet taken at gunpoint and was ordered to drive his attackers, two 16-year-old teenagers, to his bank – where they intended to empty his account. In a move he'd first seen in an Arnold Schwarzenegger film, the man accelerated away at great speed before driving headlong into a parked truck. The first robber died instantly as the impact snapped his neck while the second became trapped in what remained of the vehicle, where he remained until the police arrived and charged him with theft, kidnapping and carjacking. The driver walked away from the wreck unhurt, saved by the only airbag in the car.

ONION EATERS

An 81-year-old man was on his way to meet a friend for lunch when he was set upon by a mugger. Unfortunately for the mugger, the old man, Mr Izzie Rotterman, was carrying a very large onion (he didn't trust the onions at the restaurant where he and his friend regularly met for lunch). As the robber attempted to steal Mr Rotterman's wallet, he was clubbed to the edge of consciousness with the onion and decided to make his getaway while he still could. The case never came to court because Mr Rotterman ate the onion at lunch, thereby disposing of the material evidence.

ELECTRICAL CHARGES

Police called to investigate the theft of a number of industrial-strength batteries were puzzled by what they found in the tent of a homeless man who lived near the site of the theft. The man, Neal Berry, who earned just eight dollars an hour, was found to be in legal possession of a laptop computer, cellular phone, modem, pager and high-resolution monitor. Unfortunately, he was also found to be in possession of the missing batteries. Although Berry claimed to have found the batteries, he was not too worried at the prospect of going to prison. As he told one reporter "I've never been to jail before, but there is a bright side: three hots and a cot at taxpayer expense."

POPULAR GIRL...

A prisoner in Israel has had his request to have an inflatable sex doll as a cell companion denied. The 35-year-old inmate, who has been in prison since the age of 14, argued that having the doll would reduce his desire for real women and therefore make him less violent (he is serving time for acts of extreme violence). In denying his request, the court took into account the arguments of the prison service that such a doll might cause fights among prisoners who were competing for her affections, or that it might even be used to fool warders as part of an escape attempt – an argument that speaks volumes about the prison service's view of its own employees.

MOANING MAMMA

A 32-year-old Italian man has been pleading with the police to put him in prison ever since he was placed under house arrest for his part in a failed armed robbery. The man regularly calls his local police station begging to be allowed in on the grounds that life in prison could not possibly be more unpleasant than life at home with his nagging mother. Apparently the woman has taken it upon herself to punish the man for his crimes, and does so by badgering him morning, noon and night. The police are surprisingly sympathetic in this case but are powerless to help. They have, however, recommended a particularly incompetent lawyer who has so far never failed to get his clients put away.

BAD FOR THROATS

Unwanted advice can be annoying, especially for those who still insist on smoking despite the overwhelming evidence that it does not make one look as cool or grown up as Humphrey Bogart. A man in Cairo became so fed up with his friend's continual nagging about his filthy nicotine habit that he decided to put an end to things once and for all. In a move that displays nicely the twisted logic of addicts everywhere, the man chose to do something about his friend rather than his 20-a-day habit. Grabbing a broken bottle, he ripped out his friend's throat before calmly lighting another cigarette. When, in court, he was asked for his plea, he claimed justifiable homicide on the grounds of persistent nagging.

MONKEY BUSINESS

An Israeli street trader was charged with theft after a number of television aerials disappeared in his neighbourhood. The man initially claimed to be innocent of all charges but was later found in possession of several of the missing aerials. When the case came to court he was able to show that he could not possibly have reached the locations of some of the aerials he was supposed to have stolen. While the court accepted this fact, he was eventually found guilty after his pet monkey was brought before the court and allowed to demonstrate the remarkable skills that it had been taught by the man. Apparently, the monkey had been raised from birth to climb into apartment blocks and steal whatever it could find for its master.

BACK FROM THE DEAD

For reasons known only to himself, a Hungarian man decided to put an end to his wife's incessant nagging by pretending to commit suicide by hanging. His wife walked in, found her husband swinging from the ceiling, screamed and fainted on the spot. A neighbour, hearing the commotion, rushed in to find the wife unconscious on the floor and the husband apparently hanging from a noose. She, of course, did what any good neighbour would do and began to help herself to the couple's electrical goods. At this point the husband jumped down from his swing and tapped the neighbour on the shoulder. The fright of this caused the neighbour to faint, bashing her head on the way down and killing her instantly.

POTATO PUNCH-UP

Police investigating a fight at the railway station in Kingston-on-Thames, England were dismayed to discover the cause of the incident. While waiting for a train to arrive, one of the men involved had noticed an acquaintance standing further up the platform eating a bag of chips. He waved to the man and shouted down the crowded platform "Give us a chip". The man responded by attempting to throw a handful of chips down the platform to his friend. They failed to reach him, but he did succeed in pelting several bystanders with chips. Unfortunately for all concerned, the chip-thrower was not the only person on the platform holding a bag of chips. All Hell broke loose as around ten separate fights started at once. Seven men, aged between the ages of 20 and 30, received jail sentences of up to four years each.

SEALED WITH A KISS

Two 23-year-old American men have been jailed for life for the murder and kidnapping of their business partner. While there is nothing unusual in this, the forensic evidence that put them away was without doubt some of the most extraordinary to come before an American court. During the abduction, the men had placed a piece of industrial sticky tape over the victim's mouth and tied his hands and feet together using tape from the same roll.

After they had killed their victim, they disposed of the tape by burning it, along with all the other evidence – or so they thought. The men had actually rehearsed their crime a week before the actual event, with one of them taking on the role of the kidnap victim. Police found the piece of tape that had been placed across the substitute victim's mouth and were able to get a conviction based on the villain's lip prints.

WAYNE'S CRIMINAL WORLD

What's in a name? In some cases, an awful lot of trouble. Society often judges people on their names. In England, silly, double-barrelled, made-up names can impress all sorts of people, but it's unlikely that there will ever be a King Darren. In America, however, certain names can be murder to live with … quite literally. In one year alone, a Billy Wayne Waldrop was executed for murder in Alabama, John Wayne Boyer received a sentence of over two thousand five hundred years for his part in the shooting of two bank guards during a robbery in Louisiana. Coleman Wayne Gray was executed for murder in the state of Virginia, Larry Wayne White received the same sentence in Texas (although that was probably for littering), and one Richard Wayne Willoughby had his sentence extended for murdering a fellow inmate in Maryland.

MADE UP

Police in Doncaster, in the North of England, acted well above and beyond the call of duty in their recent efforts to stage an identification parade. The alleged criminal was black, and so the police approached members of the local black community to find the required number of men needed for an identification parade to take place. To their enormous surprise, the police experienced remarkable difficulties in finding anyone who might even consider helping them. So they resorted to hiring a makeup artist to put black faces on seven white men. Even the judge found this funny – so much so that he dismissed the case and ordered the police to stop wasting his time.

VERY LONG LIFE

People often complain about criminals who appear to be let off with light sentences, but the good citizens of Oklahoma can have no such complaints. A court there quite rightly sentenced a multiple rapist to rather more than the usual 12 years in prison. This particular low-life had been given a 2,200-year term in jail. He appealed against the sentence. The judge at the appeal clearly chose to show the rapist the same degree of mercy that he had shown his victims and, far from reducing the sentence, actually increased it by more than 9,000 years. The rapist, Darron Bennalford Anderson, appealed again and this time it must have been his day, for the judge at that appeal reduced his sentence – by 500 years. Anderson is now due for release in the year 12,744 AD.

WHAT A CARRY-ON

Detectives in London, England are seeking information that may lead to the capture of a man who is using the telephone to impersonate police officers. The man, who gains no financial benefit from his actions, rings up women at random and tells them that he is investigating a very serious crime but is prevented from explaining the exact nature of the case because he is restricted by the Official Secrets Act. He then asks the woman if there are any other women present in the room. If the answer is yes, he then requests that they both stand up and take turns carrying each other across the room. When they have carried out his request he usually thanks them both and then hangs up.

FINGERED ROBBERY?

A man in Modesto, California, is to appeal against his conviction for armed robbery on the grounds that he did not carry out his crime with the aid of a gun. The robber, who glories in the unlikely name of Sam Quentin, marched into a bank barged straight to the front of the queue and demanded the usual large sum of cash. Video tape taken from security cameras at the scene clearly shows that he was not holding a weapon at this point, but had formed his hand into the shape of a gun using his thumb and index finger. Nevertheless, the cashier handed over $3,000 in cash to Mr Quentin, who was arrested by security guards before he could make it out of the bank.

FRIENDLY FELLOWS

While on trial for a series of bank robberies – and for resisting arrest – the leader of a group of white supremacists attempted to show his caring, sharing side. (By "resisting arrest" the court was referring to a case of resisting arrest with the aid of a large calibre, semi-automatic weapon, not simply failing to come quietly.) On his lawyer's recommendation, he produced two pre-operation transsexuals with whom he had been having affairs at the time of the robberies, in the hope that their testimony would get him a reduction in sentence. They testified to his previous good character and his loving, romantic nature and also added that society's condemnation of his desire to dress up in women's clothing probably contributed to his anti-social behaviour. The court was amused but not convinced.

GREAT ESCAPE

This story comes from Belgium. A particularly athletic burglar was at work in a house in Antwerp when he was disturbed by the unexpected return of the people from whom he was stealing. After an initial confrontation, he managed to push his way past the home owners and escape into their back yard. The house was one of several in a terrace, and so rather than run from garden to garden, the burglar opted to go over the nine-foot-high back wall. In a breath-taking display of gymnastic ability, the robber ran at the wall and managed to scale it in one bound before dropping down over the other side…into the local prison.

RAINY-DAY ROBBER

Just how desperate would you have to be before attempting to hold up a crowded restaurant with a rolled-up umbrella? A man was arrested by police in a cafe in Milan, Italy after he pulled the "weapon" on the assembled waiters and diners during an attempted robbery. At first everyone went along with the man's request to hand over their valuables until a waiter, who had been detained in the kitchen, walked in and began to laugh at the sight of his colleagues being held up at umbrella-point.

CALLING IN EAVESDROPPERS

In the English county of Sussex, police hit on a novel way of catching people who had been listening into the police band radio illegally. Realizing the close similarity between the kind of nerd who sits at home with nothing better to do than listen in to police radio and the kind who is waiting for the world to be taken over by aliens, the police sent out a hoax call for urgent assistance. The message, broadcast on all police frequencies, appeared to be from an officer who had seen a group of extra-terrestrials land on the South Downs. They then simply sat back and waited for their arrestable audience to arrive.

HIGH SCHOOL

It seems like childhood innocence is coming to an end earlier and earlier these days. A telling example of this comes with the tale of a group of junior school children in Canada. The children had been given homework to do but had failed to complete the tasks set for them. Their teacher had little choice but to make the children stay behind during the afternoon break and finish their homework. Having made sure that they were working away, the teacher stepped outside for a while. When she returned she found, to her horror, that the children had found another use for their homework – they were puffing away on marijuana joints rolled from paper torn from their homework books.

SMALL BEER, SMALL BEARDS...

There was a time when students would stay up half the night fiercely debating the merits of Kant over Hegel or Einstein over Heisenberg, but not any more. These days they are more often to be found propping up bars and arguing the merits of various drinks. So it was that two students in Nottingham, England – John Brown and Mike Beever – found themselves rolling around the floor of their student union after a heated debate broke down into a non-academic punch up. Things got so out of hand that the police were called to break up the fight. Later, in court, the reason for their falling-out emerged. Apparently Mr Brown was of the opinion that he had the finest goatee beard in the building, whereas Mr Beever was convinced that his was by far the better growth. Both men were bound over to keep the peace.

VIDEO STALKER

Do you ever get the feeling that you are being watched, only to turn around and discover that there was nobody there? A woman in the county of Surrey, England was troubled by the sensation that she was being watched whenever she went into her bedroom. Whenever she looked out of her window, she could see nothing and nobody nearby, only the many empty spaces in the little-used car park at the back of her house. She eventually noticed, however, that a security camera in the car park was, rather mysteriously, pointing at her window rather than at the car park. She informed the police, who paid a visit to the security team at the car park and confiscated a number of video tapes. Not only were the police able to confirm the woman's worst fears, but they were also able to catch the culprit, who had accidentally filmed himself positioning the camera in the first place.

JUSTICE NEVER SLEEPS?

It has been said of British justice that it must not only be done, but be seen to be done (to which the great J B Priestley once famously replied, "It must not only be seen to be done, it must be seen to be believed"). Priestley's observation springs to mind after reading reports that an Englishman's appeal against his conviction for fraud was rejected recently. Despite the fact that the man was able to prove, beyond any reasonable doubt, that the judge at his trial had slept through portions of the evidence, the Court of Appeal found against him and he was sent to prison for 18 months. Apparently, the distinguished panel of judges felt that the summing-up that the trial judge gave showed that he had sufficient grasp of the case – or at least the bits he hadn't slept through.

A VERY NICE MAN...

The Internet is a wonderful thing. It allows almost instant cross-border communication, it provides access to millions of pieces of information and best of all, it helps to bring people together. Women, however, should be wary when answering the lonely hearts ads on the Internet, especially if the person advertising lives in California. The Atlanta Journal published a story about the increasing numbers of prison inmates who are trying to find romance via the Net. One prisoner's ad was directed at women who were tired of meeting the wrong man and offered them the opportunity of meeting a decent, honest and caring man; a good man. That particular advertiser is currently serving life, without parole, for first- and second-degree murder, sodomy with force and kidnapping.

TAPING THE PISS

The rise of the video recorder has brought with it many benefits. We can now all squirm at the sight of our drunken antics caught on camera for the very first time, or hang our heads in shame when the video reveals that the homeboy walk we had been practising for most of our adult lives is revealed to be as cool and elegant as an overheated automobile. The camcorder has also given us a new kind of pervert – the serial video tapers. These people get their kicks from secretly filming women urinating and will go to enormous lengths, using remarkably advanced technology, to achieve their ends. One such man was recently sentenced to four years in prison after he was repeatedly caught making these films. After an earlier hearing, he agreed to see a therapist, but ended up secretly filming her. When appealing against his four-year sentence, he argued that his behaviour, though "immoral" and "repulsive" was not illegal. Unfortunately for him, the state felt that he was right in his assessment only two out of three times.

BUM DEAL

The scale of damages awarded in compensation cases never fails to astonish and confuse most people. The infliction of serious violence on a person can result in a compensation payout of a few thousand pounds, but to claim that the aristocracy are workshy and live off the backs of ordinary taxpayers is to invite claims in excess of hundreds of thousands of pounds. The level of inconsistency that can arise was highlighted by a case in America, where 13 prisoners were awarded compensation after it was discovered that the prison authorities had over-reacted during a prison riot. Five men who had been left tied up for several hours were awarded $1,000 each, while each of the eight men who were forced to undergo unnecessary rectal searches were awarded $9 each. A lawyer for one of the eight men commented afterwards that he felt that his client had been "unfairly treated", even going so far as to say that he felt he had received a "bum deal".

GREAT CONVERSATIONALISTS

Ever since the Seventies, the film industry has insisted on showing gangsters not as vicious, mean-minded individuals who make a living by exploiting the weak and the unprotected, but as glamorous figures, "men of honour" who have the brains and the courage to step outside of the accepted values of society. This image of the master criminal was exposed for the lie that it is by tape recordings played at the trial of a couple of lowlifes in a court in the USA. The jury had to stifle giggles as they sat through FBI recordings during which the two men, contract killers for the Mafia, got lost on the freeway on their way to a hit, figured out whether or not they had enough cash on them to buy bullets for their next job, and went into a lengthy discussion on what they believed their wives thought they did for a living.

BURNING PROBLEM

A keen cigar collector decided to insure his collection under his general household insurance policy. Under the terms of the policy, the cigars were insured against fire, theft and flood. He took the added precaution of keeping them in a humidor to ensure that they would always be in the very best of condition. All went well until one night when he came home drunk with a few friends in tow and decided to pass round the cigars. Before they knew it, he and his friends had smoked the entire collection. "Not to worry," said some smart Alec, "you're covered against loss by fire, put in a claim for them." Believing this to be a brilliant idea, the man did so and after some legal wranglings his insurance company did indeed pay out. The insurers, however, managed to have the last laugh – two weeks later they had the man arrested for arson.

GUILT TRANSFERENCE

It has long been a tradition among criminals to claim that they "didn't do it". Sometimes this really is the case, although more often than not it is simply an indication of the villain's inability to face up to the fact that he or she is in fact a villain. Occasionally, however, there comes along a case where you have to wonder just how deluded a person can be. A man who went on a killing spree in North Carolina last year lost his appeal against a multiple life sentence – on the understandable grounds that he did it – and so turned on his former psychiatrist. He sued the poor man, claiming that the psychiatrist was responsible for the murders on the grounds that he retired before the murderer had been cured of his homicidal tendencies.

THE LORD'S WORK

There has always been an air of rather smug self-satisfaction about the happy-clappy salespeople for religion who bang on front doors and ring doorbells motivated by a sense that they are doing God's work and can therefore do no wrong. This idea is also beginning to gather support in the courts, where an evangelist was recently given a very light sentence for carrying out a fraudulent fund-raising scheme which saw hundreds of people lose their life savings. He was able to get away with such a light sentence because the judge became convinced that the man had a delusional personality which led him to believe that he could commit any act as long as it was in the service of God.

QUICK CHANGE ARTIST

It would be a cold-hearted person indeed who could not feel touched by the obvious naiveté of a 25-year-old man from Athens, Georgia, who found himself in court charged with assault and robbery. The man had been arrested after a long car chase following the hold-up of an all-night chemist's shop in the city. During the chase, he had rammed a police car off the road and hospitalised a police motorcyclist after deliberately side-swiping him with his car. Representing himself in court he claimed, in his defence, that he had not been the driver of the car or the person who had carried out the robbery. The police had already stated that they believed the car driver and the robber to be one and the same person. Instead, the defendant claimed he had been an innocent passer-by who had been knocked unconscious by the driver of the car who then swapped clothes with him and made his getaway before the police arrived. The court was so impressed by this story that he received a jail term of only 15 years.

UNDERWRITTEN SECRETS

Underwear is something that many people do not wish to discuss with others, however this secrecy can be taken to quite unnecessary lengths. An Israeli man was imprisoned in Egypt charged with industrial espionage. It appears that the man was working in a factory in Cairo, and was accused of smuggling out factory secrets by writing them down on his Calvin Klein underwear, using invisible ink. Apparently, the person to whom he was passing these distinctly James-Bond-like secret messages confessed to his part in the crime, even though he admitted that he didn't know what it was that had supposedly been revealed.

NUMBERS UP

Life once again imitated art when a hotel porter in Bangkok – a city renowned for the quality of its architecture – was arrested for stealing valuables from the safe-deposit boxes used by guests of the hotel. There were no signs of forced entry, and management of the hotel were at a loss to explain how the porter had gained access to the boxes but were able to arrest him after he was caught on police cameras rifling through a box of jewels. After a great deal of questioning, the porter admitted his guilt and even explained how he had carried out his crime. Using a trick he had seen done previously in an American detective series, the man had coated the combination buttons on the safes with the oil and then checked to see which ones still had oil on them. The safes were secured with three-number codes and so it took him no time at all to get into the boxes.

FINGERED FOR THE ROBBERY

The development of fingerprint records for use in detecting crime resulted in one of the most useful tools possessed by police forces around the world. Fingerprints are unique and often provide incontrovertible proof of guilt. This was certainly the case for an unfortunate burglar in Manchester, England who provided rather more fingerprint evidence than was needed when he attempted to steal an entire safe from an office block in the city centre. Having failed to open the safe by means of picking the lock, the hapless thief tried to carry it out of the building to a waiting car. Using all the strength he possessed, he managed to raise one corner of the safe and had just put his hand under it when the alarm went off. In his panic, he dropped the safe on to his fingers. Driven by the need to flee, he pulled away with all his might and left behind the tip of his middle finger. Police who arrived at the scene shortly afterwards noticed the severed finger tip and had merely to do the rounds of the local casualty departments in order to find their man.

THANKS DAD

Parents generally have an uncanny knack of knowing when their children have been up to no good. One set of parents with reason to worry about what their child had been getting up to were Glenn and Doris Tyrone, from Knoxville, Tennessee, who had the misfortune to bump into their own son when they dropped into a liquor store on the way to visit friends. While queuing at the till, they heard a familiar voice demand money with menaces. Turning around, they discovered their son holding the family shotgun and pointing at the cashier. On seeing his parents, the boy handed the gun to his father and ran off, only to be picked up by the police an hour later back at the family home.

BLOODSUCKERS

Vampires have been active in Beijing, the Chinese city where the people's government put down an uprising several years ago. While it has long been rumoured that the country's political elite have been executing prisoners in order to steal their body parts for transplantation, it seems that fears over the possible contamination of the city's blood supply with the AIDS virus has created a black market in blood from healthy young people. Originally, this was seen as a way for the young-but-poor to supplement their incomes, but things have become so bad that criminal gangs have been kidnapping healthy specimens and draining them of up to three pints of blood in a single go. The story actually broke in the West after a journalist went for an interview with the vampires and came back several pints lighter.

WELL TOOLED UP

Boy Scouts are always being told to be prepared, which usually involves carrying a Swiss Army knife, a length of fish line, a hook and a box of matches. Some people, however, can take this idea too far and, for them, being prepared takes on a whole new meaning. Three robbers working on the Subway system in New York turned up to rob a newsagent's stand at the Times Square station. Between them they were carrying four semi-automatic pistols and a pump-action shotgun. Overkill, really, for stealing three Hershey bars and a copy of the *New York Times*.

CRIMINALS IN CHRIST

God may work in mysterious ways, but the ministrations of one priest probably had more to do with the Devil than God. The priest, who was finally charged with multiple instances of the sexual abuse of boys in his care, would get his young congregation to perform fellatio on him having first assured them that it was God's special way of administering the Holy sacrament. Meanwhile, over in the States, a female police officer has been dismissed for being "excessively Christian". Apparently she was unable to distinguish between ordinary wrong-doing and the Devil's work, and was found out after her commanding officer noticed the striking similarities between the text of her crime reports and the *Book Of Revelations*.

MESSAGE MANIPULATORS

Computer hackers can be sad people – breaking into someone else's system to make a minor nuisance of themselves, but the hackers who broke into the New York City Police Department's voice mail system were a case apart. Rather than simply being a pain in the butt, they wanted to protest at what they saw as the lack of effort being expended in reducing the high crime rate in the city. As a result of the hackers' direct action, anybody attempting to contact the police on routine matters was directed, automatically, to a recorded message which stated the following: "We are too busy eating doughnuts, drinking coffee and masturbating to take your call right now. Leave a message and we won't get back to you." A slur on the good name and efforts of the New York City Police Department perhaps, but an effective protest and so much better than simply wiping all the files on their computer system.

MISTAKEN IDENTITY

In what can only be seen as a paranoid act of revenge, a man took two employees of the Domino Pizza parlour in Georgia hostage at gun point. He then demanded the largest pizza on the menu to go with the $100,000 he wanted if any of them were to get out of the building in one piece. The money never arrived and the man eventually gave himself up after eating the pizza and becoming convinced that he had made his point. The incident was believed to have been triggered by an advertising campaign that Domino's had been running at the time. The campaign featured the slogan "Avoid The Noid" and referred to a red-coloured Devil-like character who ran around stealing pizzas before they could be passed to their intended owners. The gunman, 23-year-old Kenneth Noid, took exception to the campaign, believing it to be about him, and so felt compelled to take action against the chain of pizza stores.

THE REAL THING

After police in San Francisco had been observing a suspected drug den for some weeks, they finally took the plunge and prepared to move in to make a few arrests. Just as they were about to make their move, however, four men emerged from the house, each carrying a large holdall. The men climbed into a car and sped off. Police followed but were forced to enter into a chase after the men spotted them. The drug dealers charged through the streets of San Francisco throwing out plastic bags full of cocaine as they went, before a road block eventually forced them to a halt. When police opened the door to the car they found that one of the men had accidentally dropped a split bag of cocaine into the vehicle's air conditioning system with the result that all four of the men were literally covered in the evidence of their crime. A police officer commented that: "They all seemed cool about it and remained convinced that they could talk their way out of the situation".

ARMED BUT NOT DANGEROUS

Police guarding Los Angeles International Airport must have thought that they had died and gone to heaven when they arrested a man who had triggered the airport's metal detector. When searched, the man was found to be carrying a number of hand-guns, several hundred rounds of ammunition, a "Rambo" hunting knife, a pair of handcuffs, a ski mask and false police ID. Furthermore, checks on the man revealed that he was wanted in Minnesota for threatening behaviour. However, the man's lawyer pointed out that they could not hold his client because the guns he was carrying were not loaded, and the officers were eventually forced to release him after the authorities in Minnesota decided that they could not spare anyone to come and arrest the man.

BUGSY MALONE?

Children, it seems, are getting into crime at an alarmingly early age. In February of this year police were called to a school in Manchester, England after a fight broke out between a pupil and the headmaster. When the police arrived, the boy attacked them as well, causing actually bodily harm to both officers. The six-year-old child was taken away, fingerprinted and kept until his parents could collect him. Two weeks earlier police had been called to the same school after a five-year-old girl had been found in possession of narcotics, which she had been trying to sell to her classmates.

UNWANTED CHILDREN

The arrival of a new baby is normally a happy event, accompanied by much rejoicing and general merriment along with comments such as "he's got his father's eyes". However, when a couple in Saudi Arabia found themselves faced with the task of having to raise septuplets, they completely refused. It seems that the father of the babies already had nine other children to support – courtesy of two other wives – and felt that he could not manage any additional mouths on the money he made as an occasional cab driver. Eventually, the police became involved and forced the reluctant parents, under threat of imprisonment, to take the children.

IGNORANT OATHS

There's something rather suspicious about people who get up in court and swear an oath on the Bible without having set foot inside a church for most of their adult lives. Furthermore, the lack of religious knowledge among "believers" has often given churchmen much cause for concern. A magistrate in Hong Kong, who had obviously seen one defendant too many rattle off the "I swear by…" routine, decided to ask a man who was facing a charge of having sold pornographic CDs if he even knew how old Jesus was when he died. The man did not, and so the magistrate added contempt of court to the charges and jailed him for ten months.

BEAM ME UP

An inmate at the Ohio State Penitentiary filed one of the strangest nuisance lawsuits the US courts have ever encountered. The newly-released inmate filed against the state governor and around 300 court and state officials. The charge? That they had "beamed down", Star-Trek style, groups of security people to give the former inmate a hard time whenever he attempted to enter a court house. It seems that the gentleman filing the lawsuit was not, for once, after compensation from the state. All he wanted was the court to allow him to side-step the security people by granting him, and I quote "Wally-draggle, Mummery Feg Winple Soupcon-type relief".

DRUNK BUT NOT IN CHARGE

Few people would argue that laws forbidding the drunk to drive are a bad thing; some might even feel that there should be a total ban on alcohol for drivers. A judge in Ohio realized, however, that a ban was unlikely to work on the drunk driver who was facing him across the courtroom one morning. Showing an understanding of human nature that could only have been gained from years of experience, the judge allowed the man to retain his liberty, but only if he fulfilled certain conditions set by the court. First, he was to move house – to within walking distance of a liquor store – and secondly, when travelling in a motor car, he had to ensure that at least one person sat between himself and the driver. Alternatively, he was to be hand-cuffed to the passenger door of the vehicle so as to avoid any future confusion as to who was driving the car, should it attract the attention of the police.

READY, AIM, MISS

The real problem with having a Constitution that guarantees citizens the right to bear arms is that any American can walk about with a gun, no matter how incompetent they might be in the use of that weapon. It is not unreasonable, however, to expect the police force to know what they are doing. In a recent drunken driving case it emerged that this is not necessarily the case. Two police officers were suspended for 14 days – presumably so that they could go off and get in some shooting practice – after they stopped a driver for drunken driving. Having pulled the man over, they found that he was so drunk that he was unable to control his automatic car, even on the side of the road. The driver neglected to put the handbrake on so the car began to drift away from the officers while they were talking to the man, who was still sitting behind the wheel of the vehicle. They decided to stop the car in true Clint-Eastwood style, by shooting out the tyres. However, despite the fact that the car was travelling at less than five miles an hour and even though they fired 14 shots between them, neither officer succeeded in putting a bullet anywhere near the rubber.

PERSONAL WITHDRAWAL

The secret to doing any job well is preparation. Without adequate preparation matters can very quickly descend into chaos and confusion. So it was that a would-be bank robber crashed, unprepared, into a newly refurbished branch of his local High Street bank and demanded, in true Hollywood style, that they hand over all the money. To his acute embarrassment, however, he found that there was nobody there. The bank had become fully automated since he had last entered the building and all he found was a couple of service tills and a row of automatic teller machines. No one would have been any the wiser as to his antics had it not been for the security cameras fitted to each of the walls. Deciding that he was not going to get any money by illegal means from this branch of the bank, the would-be robber shrugged in the resigned manner of a man who has faced more than a few disappointments in life before, pulled out his cashcard and used one of the machines.

MISTAKEN IDENTITY

Everyone in the room listened open-mouthed as a man, convicted two years previously of an armed robbery, attempted to convince a court of appeal that he had been wrongfully imprisoned. His defence rested on the notion that reports from eyewitnesses as to the identity of the robber could not be relied upon as evidence of his guilt. Even though the man was arrested outside the bank, in possession of stolen money, and with a two guns and a knife secreted about his person – and even though his accomplice, who was arrested in the getaway car, had identified him as the man who had gone into the bank to carry out the robbery, the man still felt that he was in with a chance for freedom. His argument was "How could the people in the bank have identified me? I had a mask on when I did the job." The appeal court remained unconvinced.

PUNCHED HEADS

Two German skinheads were plotting the rise of the Fourth Reich in a snooker hall when a Cuban man walked in, racked up the balls on one of the tables and began to play a game with his friend. The skinheads decided to make him feel welcome by shouting abuse and threats in his direction. The Cuban gentleman put his snooker cue down, went over to the largest of the retards and decked him with a single punch – he just happened to be the Cuban pro-boxer, Juan Carlos Gomez. The skinheads left, having first threatened to return with others of their ilk. True to their word, they did indeed return with a posse, but this was still not a problem as far as the boxer was concerned. He simply decked the largest one again and watched as his fellow stormtroopers filed out in embarrassment, not wishing to be the next to meet the same fate.

POOR FELLOW

The US has, what can only be described as a perverse passion for divorce. It is not unusual to see people lose enormous sums of money in settlements that would be considered shocking in other countries. One aspect of US divorce law that is unusual but really rather fair, however, is the no-fault divorce settlement in which divorce becomes merely a question of finance, with the person with the most money making payments to the less well-off partner. Consequently a woman from Colorado found herself forced to pay her husband $4,000 in a divorce settlement, even though she had appealed against the judgement claiming that she should not have to pay anything at all. At the time she appeared to have a convincing case as her husband was about to begin a 12-year sentence for her attempted murder, but the court felt that this should have no bearing on the settlement and found against her.

NOT SO INNOCENT

A circuit judge revealed rather more about himself and his own tastes than he imagined when he was called upon to pass judgement in the case of a former games teacher who had been charged with making secret video recordings in the girls' changing room at the school where he worked. After retiring to review the tapes at his own leisure, the judge dismissed the charges against the teacher on the grounds that the tapes could not be said to be lewd because the portion filmed by the defendant displayed "innocent nakedness". Even the fact that the games teacher had intercut these scenes with footage from a hardcore pornographic film did not sway the judge in his, supposedly, unbiased view of events.

COME FLY WITH ME

What is the world coming to when you cannot even rely on the police to behave honestly? An airline in the US released a story about a "misunderstanding" over a ticket it had sold to a police chief in Kansas. The senior officer was due to attend a conference of like-minded individuals, and to this end, had purchased a ticket for the trip across the States. When, at the last moment, the officer was unable to attend because of family difficulties, she did what we would all do, and made up some fake police ID with her name on it but her deputy's picture where her own should have been. Interestingly enough, no one would have noticed but somebody at the police chief's own station called the airline and tipped them off to the fact that someone was about to use a ticket fraudulently.

PARENTAL CHOICE

A high school in New Hampshire kind of missed the point when parents expressed concern about a teacher who had recently started work there. The teacher, a known paedophile, had been convicted of sexual assault against an eight-year-old child. The head of the school wrote to parents and explained that they had nothing to worry about as the child involved in the previous incident had been a young girl and their school was, after all, a school for boys.

ILL-SUITED

An armed robber found himself faced with the prospect of a further 125 years in prison after he chose to present his own appeal against conviction. Acting as your own lawyer is never a good idea – probably because judges hate to see their friends done out of a fee, and also feel insulted at the notion that just anyone should be allowed to get up and address the court. In this case the defendant quite clearly did the damage himself. He claimed that he should be released from prison on the grounds that he was not suited emotionally to life in a correctional institution. He did not help his cause, however, by parading around in court in the standard-issue orange prison uniform. The judge took him to one side and was kind enough to suggest that he might have more chance of convincing the jury of his case by wearing a more conventional suit. However, the robber replied, within earshot of the twelve good men and true, that he preferred to keep his prison uniform on as he felt more comfortable in it than he did in ordinary clothes.

JUROR FOR THE DEFENCE

Convinced that he had helped to jail the wrong man, a juror in America spent a considerable sum from his own savings mounting an appeal on the man's behalf. The juror's faith was rewarded when the convicted man's alleged victim came forward to say that he had lied under oath and that, in fact, no crime had been committed. Newspapers at the time reported that this was the first time in American legal history that such a thing had occurred. They were proved wrong when a lawyer drew their attention to an appeal that had been heard earlier in the year after a juror blew his life savings attempting to free a convicted murderer he had helped to sentence the previous year.

STRESS FACTORS

The phenomenon that is road rage may be no more than a symptom of a much deeper malaise. Take the case of the petrol pump attendant who shot six bullets into a customer's car because the attendant didn't like the way the driver handed him the key to the lock on the filler cap. Or the case of the lawyer who drove his car through the window of a video store after the clerk insisted that he paid the money that he owed on previously-rented videos before he could borrow any more tapes. Sudden bursts of rage can probably be put down to stress. For instance, the person who had just had his umbrella knocked by a passer-by would not have retaliated by shoving it into the unfortunate man's eye so deeply as to cause irreparable brain damage if had just got home from two weeks all expenses paid in an island paradise.

MORAL GUARDIAN

The excuses that criminals give for their actions are sometimes so bizarre that one is tempted to accept that they truly believe every word of what they say. A 33-year-old man was arrested by police in California and charged with theft after he was video-taped stealing clothes from washing lines outside several houses in Pomona. Normally in such cases, the thief tends to limit himself to underwear, but police noticed that the man took his time when stealing from washing lines and often left the underwear behind. When questioned, the thief explained that he was not stealing for his own bizarre gratification but because he wished to protect women from the consequences of wearing clothes that revealed too much naked flesh. When police later searched the man's house, they found nearly half a ton of skimpy outfits that he had removed from washing lines in order to save their owners.

SCARY SCHOOLS

Anyone who doubts that schools are getting rougher all the time need only look at a report on incidents recorded in American schools over a two-week period in 1998. During this sample fortnight, one 12-year-old boy was discovered planting a bomb in his school, but the real action took place at a day care centre. One four-year-old brought a gun to the centre, another child used it to shoot at the centre's manager, and the older brother of the four-year-old was discovered in possession of a hit list that featured the names of most members of staff at the centre. But it doesn't end there. Three boys in the South were arrested after phoning in bomb threats, another opened fire on his school principal's office after receiving a bad report, and four children, in four entirely unconnected schools, were expelled on the same day after making death threats to one or more fellow classmates.

PIMPLY PIMP

A 13-year-old boy has been convicted of operating a prostitution racket – at his school. The court heard that the boy, who like the school must remain nameless, was responsible for recruiting seven of his female classmates into the racket – although he had to explain to most of them what the job would entail. In most cases the girls were coerced into joining his operation and it seems that even then they had little understanding of what the job involved. Having recruited the girls, our pint-sized pimp then made the rounds of the boys, offering the girl's services for a mere £10 a time. So successful was he in this that he was able to make a considerable sum of money before the authorities moved in to shut down his operation. So far police have been unable to recover any of the money as the boy apparently spent it all on "sweets and trainers".

ADDING TIME ON

A former accountant in Maryland was sentenced to four months in prison. He managed to increase his jail term by eleven years after he took to writing sexually-explicit threatening letters to the President of the United States and also to a number of highly-placed judges, state prosecutors and prison officials. He began writing the letters shortly after his first prison term began. When he appeared in court in connection with his correspondence he elected to represent himself and there, it seems, is the root cause of his problems. During his latest trial – for sending death threats to the prison governor and the governor's wife – he so annoyed the trial judge that he received the maximum possible sentence and so will not be released for very many years. Friends are now pleading with him to stop his letter-writing, or at least find himself a proper lawyer.

CHOCAHOLIC

There was a time when the notion that there was honour among thieves could be relied on. Alas, those days are over, as is illustrated by the case of a prisoner serving time in the Virginia State Correction Facility. The concept that prisons serve as places where people can go to contemplate their crimes before emerging as a wiser and better person for the experience was turned on its head when a prisoner was given the job of pushing a snack trolley from the prison's canteen to a storeroom on the other side of the building. As he walked past a locked cell, an inmate attacked him with a broom handle – rendering the unfortunate man unconscious – before stealing two packs of sweets. The prisoner who carried out the assault and theft was not difficult to detect. (He was the only one with an unconscious man outside his cell and chocolate around his mouth.) When he was taken to court over the matter he did, however, find the nerve to plead not guilty to the offence.

SMUGGLED SURPRISE

We've all heard stories of people who open shop-bought goods only to find that they contain something that they had never intended to purchase. In most of these stories, the package usually contains something unpleasant, such as a well-used set of false teeth, or perhaps the remains of a dead animal. A man who returned to Britain from America with a radio-cassette recorder was, however, definitely not prepared for what was found after he asked the staff at an electrical shop to take a look at his purchase. He took the radio-cassette player into a repair shop close to his home, complaining that several of the control buttons would not stay down when he pressed them. On closer investigation, staff at the shop discovered that this had been occurring because of an obstruction the machine had been packed with over $200,000-worth of cocaine.

EXPENSIVE MISTAKE

Police in Florida are learning to live with the consequences of an administrative error that resulted in them turning up to the wrong address to arrest a suspect. They had been hoping to arrest a gang of drug dealers – the kind who only exist in tabloid newspapers – and so turned up carrying a large battering ram and wearing bullet-proof combat gear. The address they were handed on the way to the raid stated that the people they were seeking could be found in the first house on the left. Unfortunately, whoever wrote this address down had not being paying attention when it was given to him, as the note should have said that the dealers were to be found in the furthest house on the left. Having battered the door off its hinges, the boys in blue raced inside to discover an elderly grandmother and her young grand-daughter. Refusing to accept that they could have made a mistake, they arrested these two hardened drug dealers and took them to the cells. As a result of ignoring the old lady's protestations of innocence, the police department is now looking at the wrong end of a 30-million-dollar law suit.

FALLING DOWN ON THE JOB

Some criminals offer such patently impossible explanations for their actions that it's a wonder they can walk and chew gum at the same time. For instance an 18-year-old American man was arrested, along with two of his friends, for the rape of a young woman in Utah. He pleaded not guilty to the charge (even though his friends had owned up) claiming that it had all been a terrible misunderstanding. He said that although he had noticed that his friends were holding the victim down, he had merely been passing by when someone pushed him from behind. It was particularly unfortunate that he had forgotten to do up his flies that morning because it meant that he penetrated the woman when he fell on top of her. Despite repeated efforts to get back on his feet, he kept slipping over until, would you believe it, he climaxed. The jury did not have too many problems reaching a prompt and unanimous verdict.

RIP VAN WINKLE

A man on trial on Canada for the murder of his wife was able to produce expert testimony in court to the effect that it is possible to commit murder while sleepwalking. The court seemed almost willing to go along with the man's explanation for his actions, which was accompanied in court by much wailing and a general gnashing of teeth on his part. Then the prosecution got up to question the expert witness and put one or two details of the defendant's crime to him that had clearly not been mentioned to the expert witness when the defence team briefed him. Among these overlooked details were the facts that the man had stabbed his wife 44 times and had then held her underwater for several minutes until she stopped breathing – both acts were witnessed by a neighbour. The prosecution then managed to slip in the fact that the man was also to be tried for murdering his mother-in-law while sleep-driving the 14 miles to her home before putting on gloves and beating her to death with an iron bar. The expert witness had to concede that he knew of no other case where a person had performed such feats while asleep.

LEARNING TO DRIVE

A 41-year-old man was convicted in the States recently after being found drunk in charge of a bicycle. He only came to the attention of the police after he tried to overtake a squad car on a downhill section of road. Because he had been charged with driving while under the influence of alcohol (DUI) the judge was placed in a difficult position. Normally, if convicted on a DUI charge, the man would have had his driver's licence suspended, but because he was riding a bicycle at the time of the incident, and anyway was not in possession of a driver's licence, the judge was forced to come up with an extraordinary punishment. He ordered the man to take the necessary steps to get a licence and then to hand it into the judge so that he could order it to be suspended for the following 30 days.

IN THE FAMILY

The old saying "Like father, like son" was proved to be correct recently by two stories that emerged from the pages of the US crime reports. When, in November of last year, a 41-year-old man was convicted in Texas of burglary it was with some trepidation that he made his way to prison. On arriving there, however, he discovered that his cellmate was not to be an over-developed 22-stone killing machine called Mandy, but his long lost son, who was also serving time for burglary. Meanwhile, over in New Orleans, a 71-year-old drunk driver found himself in a head-on collision with another drunk driver, aged 35. When the case came to court, with each man trying to sue the other over the incident, it emerged that the two men were, in fact, father and son – although they had not seen each other in over 30 years.

AIRHEAD

It has always been clear-cut that ignorance of the law is no defence against a criminal charge. The line: "I'm sorry your honour, I was not aware that molesting sheep was in any sense a criminal activity in this part of Wales" is simply not a valid defence. Ignorance of matters other than the law, however, can form the basis of a perfectly valid case for the defence, as one American lawyer discovered. Stupidity was the cornerstone of the defence for his client, a Mr William "Marilyn" Monroe. Mr Monroe faced a charge of aggravated burglary after he stole a gas stove. Although he did not deny stealing the stove, he refused to accept responsibility for the explosion that occurred as a result of his severing the gas supply pipe during the theft. The explosion and the resulting fire put two people in hospital with serious burns, and injured three others. His lawyer said, in Mr Monroe's defence, that his client was genuinely too stupid to realize that pulling out a gas stove would result in a dangerous gas leak.

FEEBLE FANTASIES

Criminals can come up with desperate excuses in their efforts to escape punishment for their activities. Here are two of the best examples of this much-neglected artform. A 30-year-old man found himself in court on a charge of dealing drugs. At the time of his arrest, he was found in the company of an eight-year-old boy, who was also in possession of drugs. The police and prosecution argued that the youngster was carrying the narcotics on behalf of the older man, a dealer. When asked for his defence, the man explained that he was merely the runner in the operation and that the eight-year-old boy was in fact the dealer. And then there was the hijack attempt at an airport in Philadelphia. In the dock, the man who had been arrested at the scene claimed that he had not shouted "This is a hijack!" but had actually shouted "Hi, Jack" to an acquaintance whose full name and address he had since been unable to recall. The fact that he was also found to be in possession of a flare gun and 17 flares did not, unfortunately, help to advance his argument.

GOTCHA INDEED

Who guards the guards? Well in this case it would seem that machines can do a good enough job. At a computer industry trade fair, one exhibitor, a company called Gotcha, was proud to present its new video surveillance software linked to a covert video camera system. While the Gotcha stand was still being constructed, the sales director decided to set up a hidden camera that would record the whole building process on to a computer's hard disk drive. The plan was to generate photographs as gifts to pass around to everyone who took part and to use as dressing on the stand itself. All went well until the night before the trade fair was due to open, when someone staged a raid on the hall. During the course of the raid, a quantity of valuable silicon chips was stolen from the Gotcha stand, but the robbers failed to notice the hidden camera. This was particularly unfortunate for them as it meant that they were apprehended the next morning when they arrived to start work – as security guards for the trade fair.

ALL CUT UP

A woman in Vancouver, Canada, collapsed under the strain of unrequited love – and her mental collapse led to a charge of murder. When the object of her affections refused all of her advances, the woman – a Miss Jo-Lynn Webster – put all her faith in one last desperate act, a rather public proposal of marriage. When he still refused to have anything to do with her she finally flipped. The night of her proposal she arrived at the apartment of her loved one, fired-up the chainsaw she had brought with her, cut her way through his front door and proceeded to chase him around the flat until she cornered him in the bathroom. At this point, with the roar of the chainsaw in his ears, he proposed marriage to Miss Webster. She replied that it was "too damn late" before pushing the blade of the saw through his abdomen. When police arrived she was calmly cutting up the body and attempting to flush it down the toilet.

RUBBED DOWN

There is villainy afoot in downtown Birmingham, Alabama where two women were dragged through the courts by the city council and the police department. The women, who run a massage parlour, were originally charged as common prostitutes, until it emerged that there is no law against prostitution as such in the district in which they were arrested. (It seems that the elders of the city never got around to making it illegal in that part of town, for reasons that almost certainly had nothing to do with the location of any brothels in earlier times.) In the end, the city council had to be content with charging the women with the lesser crime of promoting prostitution – for operating a massage parlour – but were unable to bring charges against any of the women who actually worked for the two defendants.

NEVER TOO OLD

When a man from Florida, Jack Dowling, reached the grand old age of 71, he imagined that he was pretty much safe from the attentions of the law. Alas, that was not to be. During the Second World War, Mr Dowling had received an injury to his hand for which he was able to claim compensation from the US government. Every month for the next 22 years, he would put his arm in a sling and trot down to his local federal building in order to pick up his disability allowance. Having cashed this, he would then put his overalls on and get on with his regular job as a bricklayer. Over this period of time he was able to claim, falsely, nearly half a million dollars. Alas he was found out, and charged with deception. The jury deliberated for 12 minutes before finding Mr Downling guilty of fraud. The judge ordered him to pay back the money and sentenced him to four years in prison.

REALLY SICK

In an attempt to extort money out of friends and neighbours, a school teacher put out a story that she had a brain tumour. Within days, gifts and money began to flow the teacher's way and she was only found out when she underwent a medical for insurance purposes and was examined by one of the people who had made a donation. Meanwhile, a police officer and his wife raised a large sum of cash from their neighbours by claiming that their seven-year-old daughter was suffering from a rare form of cancer and was in need of an expensive bone-marrow transplant. Having spent all the money on themselves, they were found out when the daughter's friends asked how the operation had gone.

NOT OUT YET

No amount of financial compensation could truly make up for the time spent in prison by a person who was falsely convicted and sentenced for a crime they didn't commit. In August last year, 41-year-old Michael Pardue had his appeal against conviction on a triple murder charge upheld when new evidence revealed that he could not possibly have committed the crimes. Despite having forced him to spend 24 years in prison for a crime he did not commit, the Board of Pardons and Paroles in the state of Alabama still refused to let Mr Pardue go, arguing that he had to serve time for crimes committed while in prison. When questioned by the press as to the nature of these crimes, a board official looked shifty and all but refused to answer. Further investigations revealed, however, that Mr Pardue's crimes consisted of three failed attempts to break out of the prison to which he had been so wrongly sent 24 years earlier.

LUCKY GAMBLE

A judge in the States refused to send a man to prison for robbing a casino in Albuquerque. After the crime took place and the man was arrested, it emerged that the casino had been operating without permission from the state board responsible for licensing gambling establishments. What's more, the casino was, in all likelihood, not declaring all of its income to the inland revenue service. The judge's explanation went rather like this: the robber should not be sent to jail in order to pay his debt to society because the casino had been operating illegally in the first place. To imprison the man for taking action against the casino, which wasn't paying its debts to society, would be like compensating a drug dealer for loss of earnings after his stock had been stolen by a rival.

PATENT COBBLERS

A court in Boston, Massachusetts, finally did the decent thing and dropped two charges against a student at the university who had been accused of arson. At the time of his arrest, he claimed that it must have been a case of mistaken identity. Unfortunately, in his innocence he had failed to realize that the words "mistaken identity" tend to feature quite prominently in the statements of most of the habitual criminals who are encountered by the police forces of the world. In court it emerged that the defendant bore no similarity to a man who was seen to flee the scene of the crime. Further, the one witness who had picked him out was known to be insane, with a past history of accusing people of crimes they did not commit. It also emerged that the police chose not to interview the 15 people who had come forward claiming that they had been partying with the accused at the time the crime took place. Furthermore, the police forensics department had been unable to find any trace of the fire or fire-starting materials on the clothes or skin of the student.

MEDICAL

There is a morbid appeal in bizarre stories about the medical profession. Anyone who has ever gone into hospital for an operation and not contemplated the consequences of a mistake by the surgeon must surely be an unimaginative soul. We are regularly told tales of medical disasters caused either by a momentary lapse of concentration or by truly breathtaking arrogance on the part of the medical profession. It must be a terrible temptation for doctors to begin to think of themselves as life-saving Gods and it inevitably follows that this kind of delusion brings with it a complacency, which can lead to catastrophe. In reading these stories we are, in a sense, confirming our deepest, darkest fears. I should say that I discovered these tales to be very much the exception to the rule. It is very rare indeed to hear of any member of the medical profession being praised in the press for simply doing the job to the very best of his or her ability, even though this is how the vast majority of our doctors and nurses spend their days. So, read and enjoy, and take comfort from the fact that you were not the victim.

PISS TAKERS

Urine can cure cancer was the claim of Dr Ming Chen Liau, one of 600 scientists gathered for the first World Conference on Auto-Urine Therapy. The scientists, representing 17 nations, were presented with research evidence that human urine can have healing powers. Some of the speakers claimed that it can help cure not only cancer, but also hepatitis B, influenza, diabetes and even AIDS. Although many of those attending the conference consume their own urine, most stuck with coffee at breakfast time.

HEARING AID

Next time you're having trouble hearing, give a thought to a woman in Minnesota, US, who sued her landlord for $50,000 after a doctor removed a cockroach from her ear. Claiming that her landlord ignored her complaints about the bug infestation in her apartment, Maria Garza's lawyers stated that she was: "Shocked, alarmed and greatly dismayed to learn that she had harboured a cockroach or black bug in her ear for nearly a whole week".

ROPE TRICK

A construction worker in North Carolina tripped on a safety rope and fell off the roof of his local school on to a wooden post that was sticking up out of the ground below. By means of a minor miracle, the post missed all of his vital organs but did leave him with a two-foot-wide scar across his abdomen. He is now fully recovered, but has decided to work without a safety rope in future.

HELD HOSTAGE

The parents of a baby girl were unable to bring her home from the hospital in which she had been born because they could not afford to pay the medical bills they had run up. The hospital kept the girl for six months until the parents finally found the money, plus interest and other charges, after a local newspaper offered to help out.

INSIDES OUT

It's often claimed that lawyers charge an arm and a leg for their services, but it seems they will go further still. A prisoner in America, who claimed that he had been unjustly convicted of murder and sentenced to spend the rest of his life in prison, offered to pay for his appeal by selling all the internal organs he could spare, along with bone marrow and blood plasma. The lawyers seemed quite happy with the deal, but were thwarted at the last moment by the State authorities, who decided that they should take steps to discourage prisoners from paying for their defence in this way.

BIG RIP OFF

What started out as a little harmless fun got out of hand when two contestants in a tug of war competition tied the rope to their arms in order to gain an advantage over their opponents. All was going well until the rope snapped. There were around 800 members of each team tugging on the rope and so when it snapped it ripped the left arms off each of the two men. Surgeons were able to stitch the arms back on and both men are expected to recover some use in their severed limbs.

BITING THE DUST

Researchers in Canada claimed that eating a little dirt each day will keep the doctor away. Using a technique called Instrumental Neutron Activation Analysis, they discovered that dirt can contain many of the essential minerals for a healthy life, including iron, calcium, vanadium, magnesium, manganese and potassium. Anyone worried about the effect of all this dirt on their digestive system need have no fear, as some samples were found to contain kaolinite, which can cure an upset stomach. We can only suggest that readers should take independent medical advice before acting on the claims of these Canadian researchers.

GROW YOUR OWN

In the future we may all be able to grow our own donor organs. Scientists at the University of Bath, England claimed to have created frog embryos by means of gene manipulation and believe that within the next ten years their technique could be applied to human embryos. Legal problems could be overcome by restricting the growth of organs such as the heart and brain, leaving the rest of the body as a kind of living spares store.

SPEAKING IN TONGUES

Anyone who has ever woken up after a rough night to find they don't quite feel themselves will understand a little of how a Scottish woman felt on waking up to find that she was no longer Scottish – or at least that's the way it seemed to everyone else. The woman, who was approaching her sixtieth birthday, had gone to sleep possessing a Scottish accent but awoke to find that she could only speak in a South African accent. She was later diagnosed as suffering from Foreign Accent Syndrome, a complaint that can occur after a minor stroke. So far there have only ever been 12 recorded cases.

HEAVY METAL ADDICT

There are almost as many ways to give up smoking cigarettes as there are cigarette smokers to give up, but one technique is definitely not recommended. An Australian construction worker chewed his way through a metre of electrical cable a day in an attempt to calm himself while suffering the pangs of nicotine withdrawal. He must have been suffering quite badly, because this habit continued for ten years until he was admitted to hospital with severe stomach pains. Doctors discovered that lead levels in his blood were dangerously high, the result of chewing on the lead put in the cable to make it more flexible. The man is now, uniquely, suffering from the dual symptoms of nicotine and lead withdrawal.

HEAD CASE

Frenchman Pierre Pumpille proved just how far some men will go to impress women when he repeatedly head-butted a stationary car, causing it to move nearly two feet along the road. As he explained from his hospital bed, "The women, they think I am a god." There were no female witnesses to the event available at the time of writing who could confirm his interpretation of their views on him, but quite a few were heard to mutter "Oh, God" when they observed his antics.

AIRHEAD

Anyone who has ever been into hospital to have a piece of themselves removed knows only too well the fear that the surgeon might make a mistake and remove the wrong piece. Unfortunately, in the case of a man admitted to a hospital in New York, his fears became a reality – a reality made all the more dreadful by the fact that he was in for surgery on one half of his brain. The chief of neurosurgery at the hospital had, astonishingly, failed to check the man's medical records thoroughly, and so ended up hacking into the wrong side of his brain. The surgeon has since been removed from his post.

RIGHT HAND MAN

A man in Norfolk, Virginia, cut off his own hand and would not let a doctor attempt to reattach it. Claiming that the hand had become possessed by the Devil and, quoting the biblical verse "If thy right hand offends thee, cut it off and cast it from thee", he got busy with a saw. When the doctor tried to reattach the hand, the man claimed that the number 666 – commonly believed by certain Christians, horror writers and the insane to be the mark of the antichrist – had appeared on the hand and refused to allow the doctor to perform the operation.

AUTO-BOBBITT

A 67-year-old man was taken to a hospital in the Bronx after his penis was hacked off by a prostitute who had taken drastic action when her client told her he was unable to pay for her services – or so the victim told the police. The next day, however, he changed his story and admitted to the investigating officers that he had actually been building a guitar when his knife had slipped and a most unfortunate accident had occurred. He explained to the police that he left his severed member on the work surface in his kitchen, where it had deteriorated to the point where it could not be sewn back on. He told police that he had made up the prostitute story for fear that they would otherwise have thought him insane and placed him in a mental institution.

BLOWN OFF ... UP ... AND AROUND

A disturbing new craze is sweeping Thailand, where the country's youth have been indulging in a bizarre practice called Pumping. This involves placing the nozzle of a bicycle pump up one's rectum and pumping away until a huge rush of air escapes to the enormous amusement of anyone called to witness the act. As with any new and potentially dangerous craze, there is always someone who has to take it that little bit further than everyone else: step forward 13-year-old Charnchai Puanmuangpak. Not content with using a two-cylinder foot pump, the boy assembled a crowd at his local garage to watch him place the end of a compressed air hose up his backside. As soon as he felt that he had everyone's attention, he dropped a coin into the machine and sent a huge rush of compressed air up his back passage and reaped the inevitable consequences of his actions. A spokesman for the Nakhon Ratchasima Hospital told a reporter later: "One woman thought she was watching a twilight firework display and started clapping. We still haven't located all of him."

CRACKPOT CRACK SHOT

Some people are born to suffer, others have suffering thrust upon them and some even choose to suffer. Mr Phil Horner is definitely a man who chooses to suffer. In 1996, an ambulance was sent to collect Mr Horner after what appeared to be a shooting accident. On closer investigation, it emerged that Mr Horner had actually shot himself in the shoulder with his own gun simply in order to see what it felt like. Less than a year later, the very same ambulance crew was called out to the same Mr Horner after he'd shot himself deliberately for a second time. When asked why he had done so, Mr Horner replied "I wanted to see if it hurt as much as it did the first time."

HARD-FACED

Businessmen in New York City are queuing up to be injected with the bacteria that cause botulism after dermatologists discovered a curious side effect of one of their newer treatments. Some of the city's skincare experts have been treating the wrinkles of rich older ladies (and gentlemen) with injections of the bacteria, which causes a temporary reduction in the sensitivity of the nerve endings at the surface of the skin. This means that the skin does not move as much as it might and, therefore, is less prone to wrinkle. Now businessmen are having their entire faces injected with the stuff on the grounds that it helps them to keep a poker face during difficult negotiations.

ALAS, POOR SICK YORICK

A fireman in America, who was sacked from his job after taking enormous amounts of sick leave, won his appeal for unfair dismissal. The fireman, the improbably named Mr Yorick Brown, won his case on a technicality and was not only reinstated in his previous position, but was also awarded back pay and pension rights for the time he was not at work – almost two years. Mr Brown was due to return to work on February 15, 1998, but failed to show up after calling in sick.

KISS OF DEATH

A medical journal in Russia has reported the first known case of the transmission of HIV through deep kissing. Normally the disease is transferred during unprotected sex or when addicts share needles, but in this case the couple were simply enjoying a good snog. What is perhaps most remarkable about the case is that the couple managed to pluck up the courage to kiss each other in the first place. The report notes that, at the time of transmission, the man was suffering from a gum disease which had caused him to loose a significant number of teeth, was displaying visible canker sores and had hair-like growths on his tongue. The woman in this case was suffering from bleeding gums and "remarkably large" cold sores.

MICE PUMPING IRON?

Medical rsearchers at John Hopkins University in America have been doing their bit to improve the lot of humankind by breeding a race of supermice. By messing about with the genetic code of the hapless rodents, they have so far been able to create mice that are twice the usual size. The researchers believe that they will soon be able to do the same for other creatures, such as cows and pigs.

PARENT POWER

A rather unusual custody battle took place in California, where a judge was called upon to make a ruling on who should be the guardian of a surrogate baby, temporarily given the name Damien. The child was carried for nine months by a surrogate mother who became pregnant artificially after a donor egg was fertilised in a test tube using donated sperm. All went well until the would-be parents of the child (who actually donated no genetic material whatsoever) decided to divorce before the baby was born. Because of the divorce, neither "parent" felt able to look after the infant and each sued the other claiming that they never wanted the baby in the first place. The judge ruled that they were "parents" by contract only and as long as everyone had been paid, they were not obliged to raise the child as their own.

BRAINLESS GANGSTER

The Kray twins once exercised incredible power in the East End of London, England. They set up an empire of crime and policed it with a level of viciousness not previously seen in Britain. The Krays eventually ended up in prison, where Ronnie Kray died in 1995. Shortly after his death, however, the Home Office – part of the British government – stepped in and removed Ronnie's brain and sent it off to be pickled by a very strange group of people in Oxford who carry out research into why people commit crimes. Had they done this while Ronnie was still alive, the Home Office would quite rightly have been accused of behaving like the Krays. Because they took the trouble to wait for him to die, they could not be accused of behaving like common gangsters. Or that's what they thought. Unfortunately, Ronnie's wife found out about what had happened and played hell with them until they handed the brain back.

DR NAG

No civilized person would claim that violence is the best response to nagging, no matter how extreme the provocation. There are times, however, when a certain cruel irony manifests itself in an act of violence. One such case is that of a man in Manchester, England who decided to get himself a co-tenant. While there is nothing unusual in that, his motive for doing so was not the normal one. As a psychologist, and for reasons that are difficult to fathom, he wished to study the effects of constant nagging on his tenant. He chose for his subject a carpenter of mild disposition and a definite willingness to pay the rent. For two months the unfortunate man was subjected to continuous nagging – morning, noon and night – which gradually ate away at his sanity. The psychologist was feeling very pleased with himself until the day he pushed things too far and the tenant responded by smashing the psychologist's head in with an axe. Although fully recovered, the psychologist now restricts his experiments to rats.

HIRED HELP

A visit to hospital for surgery can be a very scary thing, particularly if you don't have complete faith in the competence of the surgeon. The case of a plastic surgeon, struck off after having being found to be negligent, will do nothing to soothe the fears of patients facing surgery. The surgeon pleaded not guilty to the charge in court and was prepared to battle to protect his "good name" until a surgical nurse revealed that the doctor occasionally brought in friends to help him with the surgery. These "friends" were usually people he had met earlier in the day while getting drunk in his favourite singles bar. A waiter at the bar is believed to have assisted on as many as 20 operations and, like a true friend, was more than prepared to get up in court and testify against the surgeon.

SHORT-SIGHTED CLAIM

A surgeon who claimed that his career was ruined after an accident in a supermarket car park had his claim for compensation rejected. The surgeon specialized in heart operations and was less than five years away from retirement when the accident happened. He claimed that he damaged his back after walking into a trailer – the property of the supermarket – which he believed had been badly parked. The lawyer defending the supermarket against the action was able to point out, with some justification, that any surgeon who was careless enough to walk into a trailer that was 28 feet long, 8 feet high, equipped with a smoking barbecue and pumping out loud music should not be allowed anywhere near an operating theatre in the first place.

HEART OF THE MATTER

The world is full of collectors. It probably has something to do with the temporary nature of human existence and our desire to leave something of lasting value behind when we go. Dr Jesse Edwards, an 85-year-old doctor about to retire from the medical profession, was on the lookout for someone to take care of his collection of diseased human hearts. Dr Edwards, who spent most of his career amassing his collection, ended up with 14,000 of them, each an example of one or more of the many dreadful conditions that can befall the human heart. However the collection isn't easy to maintain and Dr Edwards experienced more than a little difficulty in finding a taker. Keeping the collection in prime condition requires a staff of five people and almost three quarters of a million dollars a year.

HEARTY CHRISTIAN

Anyone out there who does not believe in the existence of God should look at a story that appeared in Berlin newspaper – a young man was stabbed while knocking on people's doors on a Sunday morning demanding prayers with menaces. The man, Tobias Vintner, a well-known and thoroughly disliked self-styled "Warrior for Christ", made a point of going round and banging on the doors of those sinners who failed to attend Church on Sunday. After several months of having his Sunday morning lie-in disturbed in this way, Vintner's neighbour answered the bang at his door with a knife in his hand, which he proceeded to plunge into the annoying man's chest. Only in hospital did it emerge that he had missed Vintner's heart because the vital organ was on the wrong side of his chest. Tobias Vintner took out full-page advertisements after this incident, claiming that he survived the attack because his heart had been moved by God. His neighbours remain convinced, however, that this miracle was, in fact, the work of the Devil.

SURPRISE DISH

A dish is becoming increasingly popular in mainland China: because of a dramatic increase in the number of abortions, more and more Chinese people are sampling the delights of fried foetus. The foetus traditionally plays a part in Chinese herbal medicine, but it is becoming increasingly common to find it on to the tables of the wealthy and well-connected. Not that one has to be that wealthy to gain access to this dish. A nurse who works at a hospital that specializes in terminations claims to have eaten more than a hundred foetuses in six months.

LONG-LOST ANCESTOR

Members of the aristocracy place great store in being able to trace their precise bloodline. If it truly is the case that the further back that you can identify ancestors, the more aristocratic you become, then there can be few people in England more worthy of a title than Adrian Tegett, a history teacher from Somerset. Mr Tegett was one of a number of people who gave a sample of DNA to the Institute of Molecular Medicine, which was able to match it with samples taken from a 9,000-year-old Stone Age skeleton found in caves near the Cheddar Gorge, a few miles from Mr Tegett's home.

HAIRY PROBLEM

Just when you thought there were no more weird medical conditions left, along comes a new one to shock and surprise. The latest distressing condition was developed by a woman in Ontario, Canada who is, or so it would appear, a compulsive sock-sucker. She developed the condition in her late teens and has been unable to go to sleep at night without the presence of a sock for many years. The condition first came to light when she was rushed to hospital complaining of severe stomach pains. Fearing the worst, surgeons cut her open and discovered, to their horror, a large bezoar – a kind of human hairball – lodged in her stomach. The hairball had developed after years of sucking on socks and is likely to occur again unless doctors can find a way of curing her compulsion.

PICK A PECKER

Anyone who doubts that boys will be boys need only look at the case of an eight-month-old boy called John, who accidentally had his penis burned off during a routine operation on his foreskin. His parents, worried about the effects this might have on him as he grew older, insisted that surgeons go back into the operating theatre and turn their boy into a girl. They renamed the child "Joan" and raised him as a female. All went well until John/Joan reached his teenage years and began to question not only his sexual preferences, but also his actual sex. Suspecting that something was not right, he arrived unannounced at John Hopkins Hospital in Baltimore and demanded to be examined. Tests revealed what he had suspected all along: that he was, in fact, a boy. He continues to receive male hormone treatments and has had his penis rebuilt with the aid of modern technology.

DRUNKEN TIP-OFF

This true story concerns a man in Brisbane, Australia, who awoke after a night out with the boys to find that he had been circumcised. The circumcision had been carried out while he was unconscious from the amount of alcohol he had drunk, although "drunk" is in an inadequate word to describe the state this man must have been in. Without the aid of anaesthetic, his friends circumcised him using a broken beer bottle. Not surprisingly, as they were in a similar state themselves and incapable of delicate surgery, the poor man had to undergo another operation – this time at the hands of professionals – in order to correct some of the damage his friends had done. The case eventually reached court after one of the man's drinking partners was charged with unlawful wounding. The judge presiding found himself unable to say much beyond the fact that he found the case "puzzling".

DOING COLD TREKKIE

According to the *Times*, one of Britain's newspapers many Star Trek fans are suffering from severe mental problems. Apparently, as many as 10 per cent of fans would be classified as addicts if their obsession were with alcohol or drugs. Severe Star Trek addicts have been known to suffer from classic withdrawal symptoms at the end of a run of the TV series, and cases of violence have been reported when fans have come to blows on the merits of The Next Generation over the original series. However, because the addictive "substance" has the veneer of respectability about it, very few such people are able to receive any kind of medical support for their non-trivial problem.

NOSE JOBS

Many people, as they approach retirement, must look back on their lives and take stock of their achievements. With this in mind, a retiring ear, nose and throat specialist from Manchester in England decided to sit down and make a list of all of the things he had removed from the various facial orifices of the thousands of patients he had seen over the years. Aside from the usual bits of pens and pencils, he was able to list a small screwdriver, a current driving licence, an old sixpence coin, and a used condom which had somehow become trapped in the nasal cavity of a pensioner from Wigan.

HEAD CASE

Anyone who has ever had to suffer that annoying expression used by the terminally cheerful – "Chin up, it might never happen" – will understand the relief felt by a woman in London, England who recently underwent an operation to correct a spinal disorder that caused her to gaze permanently at the ground. The 17-hour operation involved removing her entire head, with the exception of the spinal cord, essential blood vessels, and the skin holding her face to her neck. A wedge-shaped slice of bone at the base of her skull was then removed before bolting the whole lot back on with a metal plate and a couple of screws. The woman made a full recovery.

CRACKED FATHER

It's good to know that some parents like to instil values in their children, give them a sense of right and wrong, and help them with occasional bits of timely advice. These thoughts come to mind when hearing the tale of a father in New Jersey who was arrested after his ten-year-old daughter was brought into casualty suffering from an overdose of crack cocaine. According to the police report, the father had believed he had been acting in the girl's best interests by showing her the difference between good crack and bad crack. He got her to smoke both so that she could experience for herself the benefits of good quality rocks – he hoped that she would be able to avoid getting ripped off in the future if she were taught the difference at an early age.

BACK TO BASICS

If you've ever had to spend an evening in the company of a psychotherapist and listened to the English language being tortured with talk of "issues around issues" and being spouted annoying platitudes, then you may feel a warm glow on reading the following story. A Canadian man, a recent PhD graduate in philosophy, decided to set up a practice as a counsellor after suffering through just such an evening. Shocked by the appallingly low intellect of the psychotherapist he encountered, he decided to ignore the usual psychobabble of people who read books with titles such as "Hey, It's Great To Be Dying" and chose instead to apply the far more demanding logical reasoning of Aristotle and Socrates. Charging $50 an hour, he leads his clients through their problems by teaching them the difference between good reasoning and bad reasoning.

NO LONGER ALL THERE

An alarming new trend in theft has led to people in the city of Las Vegas becoming increasingly unwilling to accept drinks from attractive strangers. One young man who did was surprised when the beautiful woman who had bought him his drink invited him back to her suite. He lay down on her bed while she went to the bathroom "to slip into something a little more comfortable". Stretching out on her pillows, the young man was surprised to find that he was suddenly very tired. Imagine his horror when, on waking, he discovered that one of his kidneys had been surgically removed.

GASSED TO DEATH

The phrase "silent but deadly" became the literal truth when a man managed to fart himself to death in a small apartment in Birmingham, England in 1996. According to the coroner's report, the man appeared to exist on a diet of beans and root vegetables. This recipe for disaster was further compounded by the fact that his tiny, single-room was very poorly ventilated, partly due to the man's attempts to insulate the room against cold winter drafts. His landlord, who discovered the body, was taken to hospital for treatment after inhaling large amounts of methane while attempting to revive his tenant.

UNCLEAN, UNCLEAN

Two English friends once shared a flat. One of them came from Manchester while the other was a Londoner. The Mancunian was not particularly bothered about personal hygiene, a situation that was not helped by the fact that the bathroom did not contain a bath. The standing joke was that both friends went home to their parents' houses for baths – the Londoner once a week and the Mancunian once a term. Research from the University of Bristol, however, suggests that Mr Manchester was actually taking the healthy option by bathing infrequently. It seems that children who take regular baths are 25 per cent more likely to develop asthma and related allergies in later life staying too clean prevents their immune systems from developing resistances, it seems.

IN SICKNESS AND INEBRIATED

An addiction clinic in London became incredibly busy after offering counselling to those members of the community who were obsessed with helping others. Out of the 500 patients from the London area that they saw in a six-month period, the most prominent group appeared to be women who compulsively married alcoholics in order to wean them off the demon drink. For the women involved, the alcoholic marriage is usually a temporary one as the husbands either die as a result of their addiction or sober up, at which point the women tend to lose interest and get a divorce.

JUST BLOODED

Athletes who take performance-enhancing drugs occasionally feature in the news as a result of getting caught out by the far from dignified screening process, which is designed to detect traces of the chemicals in the athlete's urine. No matter how many times people get found out for this kind of behaviour, there is always someone who believe that they can get away with it. The woman who won the marathon at the Southeast Asia Games had no problem admitting that she took a substance to enhance her performance. When, having just won the race, she was asked for the secret of her tremendous stamina and strength, she replied that she regularly fed on her coach's blood.

PACK UP YOUR TROUBLES ...

A woman who was released from hospital was forced to contact the medical staff again shortly after she arrived home – her daughter collapsed while unpacking her mother's belongings. Patients at the hospital had been complaining about sent home with fewer belongings than they went to hospital with. As a result, a junior member of the hospital's staff had been given the job of finding everything that belonged to patients and making sure that patients were sent home with all their belongings. Unfortunately, the staff member had been a little overzealous and had performed his superior's request to the letter for this woman. When the woman's daughter unpacked her mother's bag she found an abundance of toiletries, cosmetics, changes of underwear and even a spare set of false teeth. What caused her to collapse was the cancerous bladder that her poor mother had had removed, packed neatly into a clear plastic bag and, in case there should there be any doubt, with a label on the side clearly stating what the bag contained.

UNREASONABLE DEMANDS

A young mother in Canada took out a multi-million dollar lawsuit against a hospital for failing to make her recent childbirth a painless and pleasant experience. The woman explained that although she knew that the anesthetist would be unable to render her totally unconscious in case her baby was harmed, she had at least expected the levels of pain to be reduced to a point where she could read a book or do her knitting while the birth was taking place. Any suggestion that she might be being unreasonable was dismissed with the words: "I am a person, you know. I have a right to expect these things".

MISCELLANEOUS

As a schoolboy I was given the unenviable task of writing a 1,000 word essay on the following subject: Describe the contents of the inside of half a tennis ball. The task was set as punishment for some misdemeanour. That essay comes to mind as I write the introduction to a chapter headed Miscellaneous. In order for a story to end up in this chapter it had to possess two qualities. As with every other tale in this book, it had to have a bizarre quality to it but it also had to be so unusual as to be unsuited to any other chapter in the book. In many respects this has produced what is probably the most interesting set of stories. There are no themes here, simply page after page of examples of bizarre behaviour. Be it the man who took to the air in a garden chair or the woman who killed her husband with a coffee pot, all of life is here. May God help us all.

ARMCHAIR PILOT

A man in Los Angeles made the headline news when he decided to go for a flight in his garden chair. Having first anchored the chair to the bumper of his car, the man attached several helium-filled balloons to its armrests. Believing that he would level off at around 30 feet, he detached the rope securing the chair to the car and took to the skies. He did level off, but not at 30 feet. A pilot approaching Los Angeles International Airport radioed in that he had spotted what he believed to be a man sitting in a garden chair at 16,000 feet above sea level. The man was eventually towed down by helicopter and charged with violating commercial airspace. When asked why he'd done it, the man replied: "Well you can't just sit around."

SHOW ME THE WAY TO GO HOME

New towns tend to look the same: row after row of identical, rather dull houses. So pity the man in Oslo, Norway who, having just moved into his new house, decided to head off in search of entertainment. He eventually found a friendly-looking bar and proceeded to drink himself into a stupor. All was going well until he decided to head for home. Once outside, he realised that he could not remember his address. Believing that he could retrace his steps, he set off in search of his new house. The police were eventually called after residents of the town called in during the early hours of the morning to report a stranger they had seen wondering aimlessly around sobbing to himself and asking anyone who would listen if they knew where he lived.

THE REAL THING?

New Yorker Frederick Koch became so fed up with people mispronouncing his surname as "Cotch" rather than "Coke" that he decided to change his entire name to Mr Coke-Is-It. All went well until the Coca-Cola company got wind of the change and decided to take him to court in order to stop him using their advertising trademark. The case, which could take as long as a year to resolve, is listed in the court files as "It, Coke-Is (AKA Frederick Koch)." In the meantime, Mr Koch is rumoured to be considering yet another name change, this time to Mr Hokey Cokey, In Out Shake-It All-About.

JUST CUT IT

Proof positive that you cannot fool all of the people all of the time comes with the true tale of a Nike television commercial which was filmed in Kenya with the aid of the Samburu tribesmen. As the commercial closes, the camera focuses in on a tribesman who utters something in his native language, Maa. At this point, Nike thoughtfully provide the translation "Just do it" which, coincidentally, just happens to be the Nike slogan. Unfortunately, when the commercial was aired on primetime American television, an anthropologist from the University of Cincinnati just happened to be watching and was not slow to point out that the tribesman is actually saying "I don't want these. Give me big shoes."

FROZEN OUT

Some couples seem to suffer from an inability to share their problems, talk through their differences and generally work together to make each other's lives that little bit happier. Eventually, this can lead to divorce, but a man in Spain decided to take things a little bit too far. Unable to express his deep unhappiness with the way his life was going, and feeling cheated because the lovely woman he had married had ballooned to the extent that she could have made two lovely women, the man decided to commit suicide. He finally took the trouble to communicate his unhappiness to his wife – in writing. Waiting until she had gone away on holiday, he climbed into their freezer and froze to death with a note around his neck which read “See if you can chew on this!”

DEATH BY ARGUMENT

Cairo, Egypt has been the scene of a couple of bizarre deaths recently. The first concerned a landlord, who, on discovering that his female tenant was unable to pay her rent, felt duty bound to pull her hair. She fought back, biting his leg in the process. As she did so, his blood pressure dropped and he fainted. This seemed to bring on a heart attack, and the man died on the spot. Elsewhere in the city, an argument over whether a young boy’s parrot had been dyed green or not, led to the death of another man. The boy’s parents were arguing about whether or not the bird’s bright colour was for real when the wife threw a coffee pot at her husband, hitting him on the head. He lay down, complaining of a headache, but never got up again. His wife was arrested only after she tried to obtain a burial permit for her husband.

MUTTON VEILED AS LAMB

An Egyptian man filed a complaint against his new in-laws after discovering, on his honeymoon, that he had been tricked into marrying the wrong woman. He had been expecting to find his lovely 18-year-old fiancé waiting for him when he arrived at the hotel but was horrified to discover that the thick veil his bride-to-be had worn at the ceremony had, in fact, been hiding his fiancé's spinster aunt, who was almost 40. Although the shock of finding that he had been cheated caused him to faint, the man regained consciousness soon after and went straight to the police in Cairo.

IT'S NOT IMPORTANT, MAN

Certain activities in life are doomed to failure before they even begin. One prime example of this is a competition that was held recently in Spain between 40 growers of marijuana. Despite the best efforts of the judges, before the competition was even half-way through, they were simply too stoned to tell whose dope was the finest. Such was the potency of the weed on offer that all taking part gave up attempting to pass judgement and instead got on with the business of chilling-out and deciding whose turn it was to go for pizza.

DRINK AND DRIVE

A train conductor in France, who'd had rather too much to drink one lunchtime, was not the slightest bit put out when he realized that he had failed to open the doors of the train at an earlier passenger station. He simply reversed the train back to the station and invited everyone to climb on board. Station staff informed the police about what was occurring, but it took them over an hour to talk the conductor into giving himself up. As he was being dragged away, the conductor protested that his drinking never normally bothered anyone.

CAN IDIOTS READ?

In an attempt to stem the rising tide of nuisance lawsuits, manufacturers in the States are beginning to put idiot-proof warnings on their products. From now on, beach towels will carry a warning that they provide insufficient protection against hurricanes, hair-dryer users will be advised against using them in their sleep and the makers of a cardboard sunscreen for car windows will warn its customers to remove the screen before attempting to drive off.

SURPRISE DEPOSIT

A grandmother in Albuquerque was most surprised to find herself staring down the barrel of a gun after handing over some cash and a deposit slip to the teller at her local bank. She was marched off in handcuffs, with her daughter, but was later released when police realized what had happened. Apparently, some joker had written "Hand over all your cash, I have a bomb" on the back of the deposit slip before putting it back in the pile. Readers are respectfully requested not to try this in their local bank.

GETTING PHOBIA LICKED

There is cruel irony in the story of the mail sorter from New Zealand who also happened to be an arachnophobe (and not just terrified of spiders but most other creepy-crawlies). The mail sorter had to be sent on special sick leave after the issue of postage stamps featuring a picture of a katipo, a truly scary poisonous spider whose bite can prove fatal. The woman has since begun therapy for her condition, but is still prone to running off screaming in terror whenever she sees one of the new stamps.

OVERKILL

There could be little doubt as to the cause of death when a man's body was discovered by police in Marseille, France. The officers, who arrived on the scene after receiving reports of gunshots, found a man's corpse riddled with bullets. Close inspection revealed that the man had been shot in the stomach, the wrist, the groin, the throat, the mouth and the brain. French police are treating this as a suicide and are not seeking to question anyone else in connection with their inquiries.

LOST PROPERTY

An Australian man who telephoned the New York Times in order to place an advert to sell part of the crashed Skylab space station was, quite sensibly, treated as a crank. When NASA received a similar call, they simply hung up on the man. Alas, for all concerned, he was telling the truth. Mark Grewar, a sheep farmer on the Nullarbor Plain had spotted the two metre-long titanium oxygen tank but didn't take much notice of it until he realized that it was not rusting, as ordinary metals would have done. Perhaps by way of revenge, the Australian government fined NASA $200 for littering.

VIRTUAL RELIGION

Anyone who feels a sense of unease when erasing a computer file, deleting a redundant application or simply binning a project that did not get off the ground need worry no longer. A Buddhist monk in Japan has created a virtual temple on the Internet (www.thezen.or.jp) and intends to hold memorial services for the dearly departed and failed to get started. Shokyu Ishiko, high priest of the Daioh Temple in Kyoto has dedicated the temple to Manjusri (the Buddhist incarnation of wisdom) and will also be offering spiritual counselling on Web-related issues. In the meantime, the Catholic Church is no doubt planning to hold bring-and-buy-sales via the Net and will be seeking to create a repair fund for its virtual steeple.

A LITTLE BIT OF YOU

For some people, owning a signed photograph of their favourite pop star is simply not enough. Fans have been known to pay small fortunes for locks of hair, discarded items of clothing and even used bedsheets that were once slept in by their idols. Now a company called StarGene has gone one better and will soon be offering photographs of famous musicians with samples of the star's DNA coated on to the paper. They hope to gain the cooperation of the stars by offering them a share of the profits in return for a little of their genetic material. Fans are said to be eager to seize the opportunity to get into their favourite star's genes.

CRACKLE AND POP

Anyone looking for a novel pre-dinner cocktail need look no further than Japan, where a steel company has come up with a wonderful gimmick – crackling ice. The ice was discovered after researchers brought back samples from the Antarctic and just happened to place some in an alcoholic drink. Air bubbles, which were trapped in the ice thousands of years ago are released as the ice melts in the alcohol, making a distinctive crackling sound. The stronger the alcohol, the louder the crackling. In tests, neat whiskey, which is around 40 per cent proof, was found to cause the ice to produce a crackling sound that registered around 70 decibels every second or so.

ONE TURD OR TWO, SIR?

The captain of a passenger flight from Buenos Aires to New York was forced to suspend the in-flight catering service after a passenger became upset when refused further alcohol by a stewardess. The man, a senior executive with an insurance company, became so incensed that he knocked over the stewardess and headed off to the first-class section of the aeroplane in search of more booze. When he was refused, he dropped his trousers and took a dump on the service cart, using napkins for paper and then wiping these all over the aircraft. No surprises, then, that the captain suspended the food service for fear of infection.

BUTT-BUSTERS

The squeamish among you may choose to look away at this point, as we reveal an astonishing and disturbing set of records that are unlikely to appear in any book published by the good people at Guinness. Establishing an unlikely sounding record, the longest turd ever recorded was that produced by an American man, who spent two hours and twelve minutes creating a monster measuring twelve feet two inches in length. And just for the record, the widest turd in history was measured at four and a half inches in diameter. While staying with matters lavatorial, the record for the longest recorded fart in history is held by a man from London, England, who managed two minutes and forty two seconds. Just who authenticates these records remains a mystery as does the necessary academic qualification for the job.

SPEED COP SURPRISE

Two officers from the Lothian and Borders traffic police in Scotland were out playing with their new radar gun on the Berwickshire Moors, catching speeding motorists and having a jolly time handing out tickets when the gun suddenly jammed up, giving a reading of 300 mph. For a moment duo were terribly confused, wondering who on earth could be driving at that speed. Suddenly, all became clear when a very low-flying Royal Air Force Harrier jet skimmed the top of their police car. The officers complained to the local RAF station, saying that their new toy had been ruined by the pilot's exploits but were surprised to find themselves being reprimanded for using the radar gun in such a reckless fashion. At the moment their speed gun had locked on to the Harrier, the plane's target seeker had locked on to what it interpreted as an enemy radar signal and triggered an automatic air-to-surface missile strike. Fortunately for the officers, the Harrier's weapons systems had not been armed.

FRIES WITH THAT TOO, SIR?

A plane on a flight to Florida was forced to make an emergency landing at Detroit when smoke was observed pouring out from a galley at the back of the aircraft. The pilot brought the plane down as swiftly as he dared, despite the fact that by then the cabin was beginning to fill with smoke. All passengers and crew observed the emergency evacuation procedures, using inflated slides to escape from the aircraft. Only later did accident investigators discover that what was thought to have been a blaze was in fact caused by a single beefburger which had been left under a grill after a passenger had requested it to be served "very well done".

FISH EAT MEN

There has been a dramatic drop in the price of fish at the Indonesian coastal town of Banda Aceh. But the townsfolk are not exactly rushing out to fill their freezers, mostly for fear that there may be more to the local fish fingers than many would like to contemplate. After the island ferry sank, killing 170 of the 210 people on-board, people are worried that the fish are feeding on something more out-of-the-ordinary than usual. So far, 56 bodies have been recovered, but the rest have yet to be found.

ERIC THE UNREADY

Several years ago, the local priest of the English village of Ewhurst was on his rounds making house calls to his parishioners. He had heard that a potential new member for his flock had moved into the village and so he made a special effort to go and visit him. He became friendly with the man, whose name was Eric, and on a later visit discovered his parishioner playing the guitar. The priest suggested that it might be nice if Eric would come down to the village hall and entertain the Wednesday afternoon get-together for the old people in the village. Sensing that Eric might be a little apprehensive, the priest gave him a month or so to polish up his guitar-playing skills before facing the elderly of Ewhurst. And so it was that a pensioners' group in a small English village were the first people to see Eric Clapton perform his finest songs in what was his debut unplugged performance.

THE COST OF DYING

A law firm in England, which shall remain nameless, showed a serious lack of compassion to the wife of an employee of the firm after he committed suicide: they sent her a bill for £10,000. According to the bill, most of the charge was for settling his affairs at the office, but it also included the cost of visiting his home in order to determine why he hadn't shown up for work (£1,100) and the cost of telling his mother that her son had died after she called him at the office to find out if he intended to visit her at the weekend. After coming in for a great deal of criticism in the press, the firm decided to back down... a little. They have now offered his wife the opportunity to pay in installments.

THE NAME'S BUG, JAMES BUG

Next time you get the urge to crush a cockroach, take a very close look at it first. Japanese scientists, renowned the world over for their undoubted skills in the field of miniaturization, have been fitting these armour-plated creepy crawlies with microprocessor implants which can be used to control the roaches remotely. Using minute electrical signals, the scientists have been able to guide the insects' movements and have even implanted microcameras into the poor creatures. The scientists aim to produce the ultimate in spying devices – a living, breathing remote-controlled spy camera.

STUFF YOUR ADVICE...

New York, New York may be a wonderful town, but it can also be rather cruel. This fact has even been acknowledged by the New York press, who felt it necessary to report what almost amounted to an act of kindness on the part of the city's dwellers. A 43-year-old man was preparing to commit suicide by jumping from the top floor of the Ansonia Hotel when a small crowd gathered to watch. It is normally considered good manners in New York to stand somewhere near the landing zone and shout "Jump" at this point, but someone in the crowd let the side down by shouting "Don't jump". Before anyone knew what was happening, more people began to shout "Don't jump" until the sound of their voices began to drown out the city's cacophonous traffic. Suddenly it seemed like the whole city was joined in one tremendous act of compassion. "Don't jump, don't jump, don't jump..." they chanted. Alas, he jumped.

SLOW WALKER

English employment laws quite rightly demand that any employee who is to be given the sack should, when under contract, be given a valid reason for his or her dismissal. And so it was that a postal worker in Warwickshire, was issued with a statement from his supervisor explaining that his contract was being terminated after 15 years because the steps he took while delivering mail were considered to be too short. The letter stated that his services were no longer required because he had been repeatedly observed walking in such a way that the heel of his leading foot never at any point passed the end of his trailing foot. The man is now believed to be seeking employment with London Underground.

PEDAL POWER

The Eighties were definitely a decade of greed. Companies spent millions on Old Masters and then locked them away in bank vaults in the hope that they would increase in value. Essentially, these paintings were only as valuable as everyone decided they should be, so it caused a great deal of concern when restorers discovered what appeared to be a tiny racing bike painted into a self-portrait by the Dutch master Rembrant. Close inspection revealed that the bike had been painted with the same paint as the rest of the painting and had been done in a style that was characteristic of the Old Master – the only problem was that Rembrandt had lived long before the invention of the bicycle. The origin of the bike was finally revealed by a man who had restored part of the painting in the Fifties. A keen cyclist, he had added the bike as a joke. He ignored the uproar his addition had caused, claiming that it did not matter as Rembrandt would have found it funny.

CANNIBAL BUTCHER?

Some shop keepers will go to extraordinary lengths when faced with what they believe to be unfair competition or anything else that is bad for business. A butcher in Cardiff complained to his local council when a large shop next to his own, which had been closed for some time, re-opened as a funeral parlour. Despite making repeated complaints to his elected representatives he received no joy. He decided it was time for more direct action, and set about making himself a new sign for his shop window. Alas, the poor man managed to miss the point and succeeded only in drawing attention to the possibly disturbing connection between his shop and the funeral parlour. His new sign read: "Our meat is fresher than next door's."

KILLING JOKE

Japanese game shows are a source of puzzlement for most of the population of the rest of the world. The damage inflicted on ordinary citizens for the sake of entertainment has shocked even the most ardent fans of western shows such as Gladiators, where the violence and mental anguish are largely sanitised to make the show more palatable for a primetime audience. Not so in Japan, where the latest televisual atrocity involved a young child who was brought on to the stage in front of several million viewers and made to believe that he had just heard his mother being shot. Why? To see how long it took for him to burst into tears…

WEATHER JUNKIES

Some people really should get out more. *The Chicago Tribune* newspaper recently carried a story about a report into the viewing habits of people who subscribe to the Weather Channel, a cable station offering 24-hour-a-day weather reports from around the world. While the report indicated that most viewers tuned in for a few minutes at a time, presumably until they had received the information they required, a staggering one in five of the station's viewers watched for at least three-hours at a time. The cable station described these viewers as "weather involved".

INFORMATION OR EMERGENCY?

Police in the English county of Kent are getting a little annoyed at the number of people who don't seem to have grasped the meaning of the word "emergency". Among some of the non-emergency calls being made to the 999 emergency number in Kent are requests for football results, for advice on which film a family should watch on TV, and for the numbers for local takeaway restaurants. One half-wit even used the emergency number to call the police to let them know that he was going to be late home. He asked them to inform his mother who would, apparently, "be worried sick" if they didn't sent a patrolman round to her house…

ART WILL EAT ITSELF

It has become something of a cliché to say that art imitates life. However, in New York a performance artist has taken this idea and reduced it to the simply mundane. It is not unusual to see works of art in a restaurant, but now a performance artist in the city is "creating art" by eating dinner – with a different guest each night of course. Any suggestion that this might be little more than a confidence trick is, quite naturally, dismissed as the heathen rantings of a Philistine.

SANITARY STATUE

Last summer the ICA (Institute of Contemporary Art) held an exhibition of work in London by noted sculptors that included a piece by Sarah Lucas, darling of the art establishment. Her masterpiece, entitled *The Great Flood*, was on loan from a collector who had paid somewhere in the region of £10,000 for it. One condition of the loan was that this great work of art be plumbed into the gallery's sewage system. Visitors are allowed to interact with the piece by pulling a chain, which has both a decorative and a practical purpose. After all, what is the point of a toilet (which is what the object was before it became a work of art) without a chain?

HOLY ROLLERS?

You've seen the film, you bought the book, now it's time to visit the theme park. A company in America has announced plans to open a theme park based on the Holy Land. The park, which is to be based up the road from Las Vegas, the modern Sodom and Gomorrah, is set to cost over 1.5 billion dollars. It will feature a tower block-sized statue of Jesus, an authentic replica of Noah's Ark and a "Promised Land" ride that will feature the miracle that was the parting of the Red Sea. It has not been confirmed whether or not the park will be built in six days.

HOUSE BUYING

Weddings can cause all sorts of problems for friends and relatives of the happy couple. Just what to buy the soon-to-be newly weds is always a source of worry, which is why more and more couples are resorting to the practice of wedding lists. (For those who don't know, a wedding list is a kind of wish list that sets out what gifts the couple would like to receive; as someone chooses a gift to supply, it is crossed off the list. Friends and family can then choose an item from the list safe in the knowledge that no-one else will buy the same item, thereby avoiding the infamous 17-toasters scenario.) Now a company in Silicon Valley, California, is offering a wedding list service for the truly well-off. Although the area has the highest house prices in the country, it will now be possible for wedding guests to purchase a mansion or a maisonette from the company, safe in the knowledge that no-one else is going to try and buy a similar property for the happy couple.

STUDENT SNIFFERS

Academics at an American university are keen to be the first to set standards in the field of objective odour detecting. To this end they are spending nearly half a million dollars over three years, in an effort to train specialist odour detectors – people who can have an objective response to an odour. The skills required for this task included the ability to describe a pig farmer without using words like "stinky", and a talent for being able to distinguish all of the chemical components of cow shit with a single sniff.

TIMEZONE

Are you forever losing your watch? You know what it's like, you take it off, put it down for a second and before you know what's happened it's disappeared. Well those days may soon be over. A company in California has announced a wonderful invention – they have developed a prototype wristwatch that is worn in the wrist, not on it. Using a liquid crystal display, a microchip and a tiny battery, the watch is fitted as an implant under the skin, close enough to the surface to make it readable but still retaining the benefits of being a loss-proof, water-proof time piece. The battery can be charged remotely as can adjustments to the time, which adds a whole new angle to the question: "Have you got the time on you?"

MUSICAL MAYHEM

Anyone who has ever had a neighbour who has a powerful sound system but really quite bad taste in music will feel nothing but pity for those residents of San Francisco who live anywhere within ear-shot of one of the city's parks. A 39-year-old man has taken to staging impromptu concerts using an enormous, diesel-powered foghorn which he bought as surplus stock from the coastguard. The man stands in the park and serenades the locals with the horn, which is capable of reaching sound levels of 140 decibels. The sound is so loud – equivalent to sticking one's head near a jet engine at full thrust – that the lonely performer is forced to wear not just ear plugs, but sound-insulated protective clothing as well. Unfortunately for local residents, this annoying little man is allowed by law to continue his recitals on the grounds that his horn is technically an acoustic instrument and therefore exempt from the usual restrictions in noise.

EGG SCRAMBLE

In America, the traditional way of celebrating the resurrection of Christ is to stage an Easter egg hunt. These hunts can get a little out of hand as children compete by rushing around trying to find the chocolate eggs. In an attempt to avoid the stresses involved with such a hunt, a church group in Daytona, Florida, decided to pile all the eggs in a heap and let the children help themselves. All went well with this plan until the children's parents stepped in, in an attempt to ensure that their own child or children got a fair share of the eggs on offer. In the ensuing rush, several children were trampled and several fights broke out between the parents.

JUDGED INSANE

The Judicial Qualification Commission in Nebraska has recommended that a judge be fired from his job for various misdemeanours, including lying, insulting female courtroom staff, signing court papers in the name of "A Hitler", setting unusual sums of money for bail (a zillion pengos in one case,) and personally supervising a young man's urine test. The final straw came when he set off fireworks in the office of another judge with whom he had a disagreement.

TAMAGOTCHI TALES

Many people have a deep-seated need to care for something or somebody, and virtual pets can provide the answer. However, an obsessive desire to look after these "creatures" can cause some people to behave very stupidly. A woman in France has found herself up on a manslaughter charge after she attended to the need of her "pet" while driving up a busy street, knocking a cyclist over and killing him. And a young boy in Japan, unable to cope with the loss of his beloved electronic friend committed suicide because he could not face life without his one true companion.

DIFFERENT WITHDRAWAL

A bank manager and his assistant had the misfortune to become accidentally locked inside the bank's cash machine while filling it up with new notes. There were no other members of staff around and so they opted to wait until someone came to use the machine and then call for help. Fortunately they did not have to wait long, and a regular customer soon arrived with the intention of using the machine. "Help us!" they cried, pushing the key to the vault through the slot which normally accepts cashpoint cards. The regular customer said that she would indeed help, but not until she'd had a word about the remarkably high charges on her overdraft…

AUTO BOBBIT

Homophobia achieved new levels of madness when a New Yorker went to the police with a tale of how an intruder had cut off his penis. In reality, however, the man had actually cut off his own penis – with a set of garden shears. He originally told the police that his member had been removed while he was sleeping in his living room. The police expressed doubts about the honesty of his story and when pressured, the man admitted that he had mutilated his wedding tackle in the hope of ridding himself of the attentions of a gay neighbour. The man was charged with falsely reporting an incident.

KILLING ME SOFTLY

Some people never seem to bother to think through their plans and end up simply making things up as they go along. A classic example of this sort of behaviour is illustrated by the case of a Californian man who threatened to commit suicide by dousing himself in petrol and setting himself on fire. The police got wind of what was going on and turned up at his house in the hopes of dissuading him, or at least arresting him before he had chance to light the blue touch paper. They surrounded the man's house and waited for nearly 16 hours before becoming convinced that the time had come to rush in and arrest him. Just before they were about to make their charge, the man emerged from the house. The scene went silent as everyone waited for him to say a few final words before turning up the heat. By now the TV cameras had arrived and the news networks were showing the scene live as it unfolded. The man spoke, but nobody could make out quite what he was saying. A police officer asked him to repeat himself: "I said, has anyone got a light...?"

THE BOOZE FILES

The drive to explore space was given an enormous boost recently when astronomers discovered a huge cloud of ethyl alcohol in the constellation of Acquila – a delightful region of space with a lovely view of the centre of the galaxy and ideal for commuting to the planet Earth, being just 10,000 light years away from the nearest landing site. The almost-pure alcohol forms a gas cloud that is 1,000 times the size of our own solar system and is believed to be equivalent to 400 trillion, trillion pints of beer. It must truly have been a slow day at the observatory when this gas cloud appeared on the monitors, as someone with a proper education took the trouble to calculate that this number of pints is enough to keep the entire population of the Earth in a tired and emotional state for 1,000 times longer than the Universe is expected to last.

TOPLESS TOWN

Canada is one of the few places in the world to contain a city in which women can wander the streets topless without fear of prosecution – so long as they are not doing it for commercial gain. This laudable and historic decision was made a couple of years ago after a group of women complained that it was unfair that on hot days they must remain fully clothed while men could wander around as God intended. Critics of the bill predicted the imminent collapse of Canadian society, but so far this has failed to occur. In fact, the only shirts-off related incident to have been reported happened after a neighbour complained to a woman that her son was able to see her sunbathing topless. The resulting argument saw both women up in court on charges of disturbing the peace.

RESERVOIR LOGS

The age of the video camera is upon us and with it has come all manner of attempts at producing home-made movies. While most of these are of the "What we did on our holidays" school of film-making, and more than a few of them are somewhat more personal and erotic, occasionally a true classic emerges. A film currently doing the rounds of home video fans is one that captures the attempts of three young men to stage an action/adventure story with a special effects budget around £3.20. All goes well until the scene that calls for two of the men to burst into flames. The intrepid junior stuntmen, who had clearly covered themselves in lighter fluid, duly burst into spectacular flames. Within seconds, however, one of the stuntmen can be heard to say "Hey, this hurts" at which point both of them commence screaming and begin rolling around on the floor in an effort to put out the fire. Fortunately for the viewing public, the third young man had the good sense to carry on filming.

EVERY WHICH WAY

A Frenchman succeeded in his attempt to commit suicide, but only just. Clearly not a man who took chances, he first climbed to the top of a steep cliff which overlooked the sea, tied a noose around his neck and attached the other end of the rope to a tree. Having first taken a large dose of rat poison, he set fire to himself and, just as he jumped, attempted to shoot himself in the head. It was at this point that things went awry. The bullet missed his head but hit the rope, sending his burning body plunging straight down into the sea. The impact with the water not only put out the flames, but the shock of the cold water caused him to vomit the poison out of his body. Not a man to give up so easily, he tried to swim out to sea but was rescued by the coast guard, to whom he was able to tell his story before dying of hypothermia.

IMAGE CONSCIOUS

Catholic priests from the Vatican have approached a leading Brazilian artist, Claudio Pastro, and asked him to do something about the appearance of Jesus. It seems that the Pope is less than happy with the image of a suffering Jesus and wants him to be depicted as a victorious Jesus.

MIND THE THORNS

A gardening programme broadcast on British national radio took the highly unusual step of broadcasting one of its programmes from a nudist centre. In order to help celebrate the 50th anniversary of the establishment of the Naturist Foundation, the programme makers thought it would be a good idea to go along and present the show in front of a live, naked audience. Speaking from the Foundation's headquarters in Orpington, Kent a spokesman for the programme's production team said: "naturists are interested in all things natural, including plants". When asked if the panel of gardening experts had stripped for the event, the spokesman remained silent. Any suggestion that someone at the radio station did not know the difference between a naturist and a naturalist have, quite naturally, been denied.

A LITTLE TREE TIME

Two stories concerning trees and their connection with the frailties of human relationships reached my ears. The first concerns an Indian man who pledged to spend the rest of his life up a tree after he discovered that his wife had been unfaithful with his best friend. He spent eight months up the tree before falling to his death while asleep. Meanwhile, a housewife and mother in Connecticut decided that she had spent far too much of her life being taken for granted by her husband and two children. She decided to climb a tree in the garden and stay there until the family promised to offer a little more support and show some appreciation for the many tasks she carries out on their behalf.

PRACTICAL PRIZES

Football ournaments occur partly to satisfy the seemingly insatiable desire for football and partly to generate large sums of television money for the clubs involved. Success in these tournaments also often generates huge amounts of cash in the form of sponsorship deals. No such rewards were on offer, however, during a football tournament played out in Vietnam. The winning team received a single dairy cow. The second place team got a non-dairy cow, and the third place team were given a pig and so could truly have been said to have brought home the bacon.

HIGH FLIERS

Sixties "Tune in, turn on, drop out" psychedelic guru, Timothy Leary, finally got his wish to be well and truly spaced-out when he, or rather his ashes, blasted off in the Autumn of 1997. NASA offered to perform this service for a select few, including Star Trek creator Gene Roddenberry. For around $3,000, a US company called Celestis will arrange to have your ashes treated in this way, and will even provide a video of the event for your family and friends to treasure. For an extra charge, you can stay higher for longer by having your ashes placed in an orbit around the Earth where they will remain for up to ten years before re-entering our atmosphere and burning up, so appearing from the ground to be a shooting star. It's almost worth dying for.

FISHY TALE

An elderly lady called Victoria Adams was making her way home one Saturday evening after doing a day's shopping. As she approached her house she noticed a crowd of about 30 very tall people coming up behind her. As they got closer she realized that they were, in fact, giant, two-legged, air-breathing fish and, presumably fearing that they were aliens who had landed on Earth to take specimens for use in bizarre sexual experiments, she ran as quickly as she could into her house. The story would have ended there had she not decided to do her civic duty. After calling the sheriff's office and explaining to a patient deputy that the neighbourhood was going to the fish, she charged outside with a shotgun and set about reducing the aliens to fishpaste. It was at this point that she noticed that the alien fish spoke English – hardly surprising, as they were, in fact, medical students on their way to an under-the-sea-theme fancy dress party.

WOMEN SCORNED...

The name of John Wayne Bobbit is etched forever on the minds of any man who has ever read his story – his wife cut off his penis after she discovered that he had been unfaithful. When Lorena Bobbit was acquitted of all charges in connection with her rather radical act of revenge, it seemed like open season had been declared on any man who stepped out of line, particularly in the country of Brazil. Within a few months of the story breaking, one man had his penis sliced off by his schoolgirl lover after he decided to end their relationship. Another man had a testicle ripped off, which his wife then flushed down the loo, after he drunkenly fell asleep during sex. Finally, a 19-year-old man awoke to find his wife pouring boiling oil over his nether regions after she had discovered a cigarette end that bore traces of lipstick in the ashtray of his car.

EXPLOSIVE INSECT

There is something very cowardly about the use of landmines in the fact that they can be planted and left for someone else to "find" weeks, months and sometimes even years later. And the people who laid the mines in the first place are often no longer around to see the destruction that their equipment causes to innocent people's lives. So it is particularly disturbing that scientists at the Massachusetts Institute of Technology have come up with a new kind of mine. Described as an intelligent anti-personnel device, it resembles a large stick insect and can home in on its victim. The device works by detecting sound, or body heat, and is able to crawl in the direction of its prey before exploding just before contact is made. At the moment the US army is reluctant to deploy the weapon because it is incapable of distinguishing between the body heat of the enemy and that of an American, and therefore "someone might get hurt".

PRIZE FLAW

I particularly despise those companies who insist on killing trees in order to send us bogus letters claiming that "You, yes you, have been specially selected for a place in our £1,000,000 prize draw." There is no possible justification for this useless waste of the world's resources – nor for the potential unhappiness that can be caused. It is unfortunate when the innocent and the unwary are taken in by these things, especially when, as reported by a newspaper in Florida, some of them actually spend money trying to claim their prize. One elderly man made two trips to Tampa, Florida, after misunderstanding the letters he had received from one such company. He would have made a third trip to claim his prize had his son not explained to him that he was in the grip of greed and madness and hadn't won anything.

DOCTOR VIDEOGAME

Many a parent has looked at his or her child playing computer games and been driven into a state of despair by the thought that the brat will never amount to anything other than a slayer of imaginary dragons or a defender of the Earth against the massed hordes of evil. Such parents need worry no longer. In January the Digipen Institute Of Technology in Washington opened its doors to students wishing to gain a degree in video game technology. The course, which cost just $11,000 a year, is already over-subscribed to the tune of ten applicants for every place on offer, despite the fact that applicants do actually need a knowledge of computer languages.

DAMN YANKEES

A man from South Carolina has contacted his local paper with the news that he is to forbid all northerners from ever setting foot on his land. The farmer, who still hasn't got over the American Civil War, appears to be concerned that until such time as the South rises again, no Damn Yankee will set foot on his Confederate soil. Interestingly, he defines a Damn Yankee as anyone who was born in the northern states, has resided there for more than a year, has the surname Sherman (as in the general who gave the Confederates such a kicking) or even has a name that is an anagram of Sherman.

SLAVE DRIVER

Four school kids from Oklahoma are dragging the entire state's education system through the courts after they were forced to take part in what their school called a "creative history lesson". It seems that their teacher wanted them to get a taste of life on a slave ship and to this end had the children tied up with masking tape and beaten by their fellow pupils. Most teachers would have drawn the line at the beating, but this particular teacher was clearly a bit of an adventurous soul because he then ordered that they be "imprisoned" together in a shower stall and smeared with the contents of dirty nappies in order that they get a flavour of what life was really like on the journey from Africa to the New World.

SMART BUT SMELLY

A student of astrophysics at the University of Oslo has had his appeal against expulsion from the university rejected. For the 22-year-old astronomer this was just one of many defeats he has faced in his battle to be readmitted to the university on his own terms. While the university authorities would be more than happy to have him back if their decision could be based purely on his academic record (astrophysicists tend to be very clever) the authorities will not allow him into the building until he agrees to wash on a regular basis. The student claims that a lack of soap and water enables him to get a better grip on cosmology and is to appeal to the European Court of Human Rights in a further attempt to gain readmission.

COLLECTION OF COLLECTIONS

For those of you who prefer their art with a capital F, the University of San Jose is mounting an exhibition for anyone who knows the way to their site. The exhibition, called Impulse To Collect, will feature a number of fine examples of work by people who have turned collecting into an obsessive art form. My personal favourite is a piece called Chromatic Extrusions Rodenta. This masterpiece was created from rat droppings collected after the rats had eaten their way through the artist's oil paints. Also on offer is one woman's collection of 696 used toothbrushes and another man's collections of items which feature a prominent red letter X somewhere on the packaging. For reasons not satisfactorily explained by the exhibition's presenters, the university turned down a set of slides displaying various examples of cat snot, and an ageing collection of umbilical cords.

RELIGIOUS ODDITIES

The church has a long tradition of attracting oddballs. Mostly these are fairly harmless and rather earnest men who are able to combine their desire to walk around in frocks with their equally understandable desire to do good. One has to go to the fringes of organised religions to find the really entertaining characters, men such as Rabbi David Batzri, who is currently advertising his services in Jerusalem. He specialises in blessings that are designed to save those who have masturbated from becoming possessed by devils. So skilled is he at this, that he can even save souls over the telephone. But any large-breasted women of sound virtue thinking of visiting Hong Kong in the near future will need to guard against the attentions of the self-styled Knight of God, a Muslim man who has been assaulting well-endowed females because he feels they resemble prostitutes too closely to be able to serve God.

IN LOVING MEMORY

Everyone remembers where they were when they heard the tragic news of the death of Princess Diana. All manner of people have been attempting to come to terms with the tragic and untimely death of the Princess of Wales by launching products on to the market that not only express their sorrow but also go some way towards making their own lives that little bit richer. To this end a delicatessen has opened in New York called, appropriately enough, the Diana-Dodi Corp. The Flora margarine people produced special edition tubs as their way of honouring the poor woman's memory and best of all, a group of people who insist on calling themselves poets published a book of their work in her honour. Unfortunately, the *Observer* newspaper was unkind enough to describe it as "possibly the worst book of poetry ever published".

CASSOCK CANNONS?

Things are obviously going from bad to worse in the Deep South, where a new piece of legislation has shocked even the citizens of a state that is one of the most enthusiastic in its championing of the right to bear arms. The legislation, which is still at the committee stage, is being prepared in order to protect the lives of church ministers, who fear that they might be attacked while making the usual collection as part of the church service. If the legislation goes through, churchmen will have the right to carry concealed weapons, including semi-automatic pistols, and be allowed to use them without warning if a member of the congregation so much as asks for change for a twenty.

WASH TO GO

A gentleman in France has just patented a new design for a public lavatory. The new loo, which is of the stand-alone variety now seen on the pavements of many of the world's cities, has a door that locks automatically whenever someone sits on the loo seat, but will not unlock until the water in the accompanying sink unit has run for at least ten seconds. This ensures that the great unwashed are at least forced to go through the motions (if you'll excuse the word) of washing their hands before leaving the new superloo. Ideally, the designer would like to combine his invention with a device that has just been patented by an investor in America. This American's invention is a small device which fits on to the side of the toilet bowl and performs the task of removing any unpleasant odours that might emanate from the posterior of anyone using the loo.

A LEG AT EACH CORNER

Top of the list of inventions I wish I had thought of has to be the "Six-day underwear" thought up by a Japanese company and introduced on to the market recently. This particularly nifty set of knickers comes with three leg holes, allowing the wearer to rotate the garment at the rate of one leg hole a day before turning the entire ensemble inside-out and beginning again on the other side. By employing this method, say the manufacturers, it is possible to at least get the impression of clean underwear from an item of clothing that can be worn for up to six days. They are now planning to release a pantyhose version of the invention for those ladies who are constantly get runs in their tights.

KEEP ON GAMBLING

If anyone was in any doubt as to what the state of Oregon considers to be of paramount importance, they need only look at a report of a contract awarded by the Oregon Lottery Commission for well over $100,000 to a company who will carry out a study of how best to restore the state's gambling operations in the event of a disaster of cataclysmic proportions. Should the world all but come to an end as the result of a series of major earthquakes, or even as the result of a collision with an asteroid of the size rumoured to have driven the dinosaurs to extinction, the good people of Oregon will be able to take comfort from the fact that their Lottery Commission will have a plan to get the poker tables up and running again. When it was suggested that there might be more important matters to attend to in the aftermath of such an event, the Lottery Commission pointed out, by way of an explanation for its actions, that gambling generates one million dollars a day for the state of Oregon.

ALL EARS

The ear is a fairly innocuous organ - when it functions properly we barely notice it is there. It has, however, featured quite prominently in a number of news stories recently. A Kenyan doctor re-inserted a coffee bean into the ear of a child from whom he had just removed it after the parents of the child revealed that they would be unable to pay for his services. Meanwhile, researchers at the University of Texas revealed that there are physical differences to be found in the inner ears of lesbians that are not to be found in women with more conventional sexual tastes. And finally a robber in London was caught because police were able to track him down after getting a unique earprint from a pane of glass at a house he had burgled.

WHO ATE ALL THE PIES?

When I was a school boy, a complete psychopath who was employed to teach in the mathematics department drummed into me and all other small boys in his far from tender care the significance of pi (which, for those who were fortunate enough to escape such an education, is a constant which never changes its value and is equal to three and one seventh, twenty-two over seven or three point one four two). I've never had to apply this knowledge in my daily life but it was so severely beaten into me that I shall never forget it. So it was that my heart missed a beat on hearing that March 14 has been declared national pi day. On this day some very curious people will gather to sing songs in praise of pi, recite poems to its honour and (it must have taken them days to think of this one) even stand around and eat pies. I can only assume that worship of an irrational number – which pi also happens to be – can bring on this kind of behaviour.

PRUDISH SOFTWARE

A software developer has produced an application that will monitor your television's output for "rude, offensive or downright obscene words" and mute them whenever they are spoken. Starting with just the seven key words that self-appointed television watchdogs object to, our technical genius went on to add another 93, bringing up to 100 the number of words that could, if used together, bring about the end of the world as we know it. So good is the latest version of this software that it not only mutes the words, but flashes up a more acceptable version as a sub-title across the bottom of the screen.

PUSHED TOO FAR

James Booth was a man at the end of his tether – life had dealt him too many raw deals. Until one fateful day when he decided that enough was enough and he was not going to take this kind of treatment anymore. The straw that broke the camel's back was a particularly bad week in court. One Monday afternoon, Mr Booth was informed by the court that he must sell his lakeside house and split the profits with his wife, who had left him for a neighbour without so much as saying goodbye. Two days later, while still contemplating the court order compelling him to sell, he was further informed that his beloved motor launch was to be confiscated in the event of his failing to put the house on the market by the end of the week. Mr Booth walked out of the court, hired the largest truck he could find and proceeded to drive at great speed in the direction of his house, pausing only to shift up a gear before jumping out of the vehicle as it ploughed through the front of the building, damaging it beyond repair. He then went to his motor launch, and set in motion an enactment of a Viking burial. The police arrived just as the fuel tank caught fire and blew the boat into a thousand pieces.

MAILMAN

A film company in Hollywood has announced a new project that is sure to have people rushing to their local cinema when it is released next year. The film, which has been described by its backers as a "thrill a minute festival of comic action and romance" (qualities to which the makers of all Hollywood films seem to aspire), is to feature, as its hero, a postman. When asked why he was making a comic-action-adventure film about the activities of the British postal services, the director of the film narrowed his eyes and replied: "Because it's never been done before". So far the project has failed to attract any big stars.

DO IT IN YOUR OWN TIME

The Occupational Safety And Health Administration in the US has been taking evidence from workers who, it believes, are being denied their basic human rights – in this case the right to visit the loo during working hours. In the course of their investigations, they heard evidence from employees of a poultry factory who were told that they would no longer be allowed to visit the toilet during the working day, despite the fact that they were expected to attend work for up to ten hours at a time. In order to get around this problem, many staff members had taken to not drinking during the day, but this had caused a few of them to faint, leading to a loss of production and wages, and even dismissal. Things had become so bad at the factory that a number of the employees had actually taken to wearing nappies to work in an effort to avoid these problems.

A WONDERFUL SON

This should serve as a warning to all those parents who insist on teaching their children "the value of money". A woman in York has begun legal proceedings against her son after he refused to share the proceeds from a winning lottery ticket with her. For the last two years, mother and son have each been putting in £20 per month to buy lottery tickets, which the son would pay for and pick up every Saturday before going to work. One particular Saturday evening he rang his mother to say that they had won two million pounds on one of their tickets. The mother was thrilled to hear this and spent the evening deciding on what she was going to do with her share. Imagine her disappointment when, the following morning, her son called to say that he had made a mistake and that the winning ticket had in fact not been one of theirs, but one that he had bought on his own.

KEEPING A LOW PROFILE

We were all raised with tales of undercover agents, and at some stage most of us have fancied ourselves as potential secret agents. Some people, however, are just not cut out for the job of keeping a low profile and behaving inconspicuously. David Waters for instance, was on the run after a parole violation, when he had the misfortune to take a cross-country flight and end up in a seat in the same row as his parole officer, who was on his way to a convention in the company of 26 police officers. Similarly unfortunate was Mr Matthew Johnson of New Hampshire, who had convinced his employer that he was unable to attend work because of a back injury and was drawing sick pay. Not for long, however, because millions of people, including his employer, saw Matthew punch a fellow guest on a live, prime time television talk show. Finally, in this roll call of the conspicuous, Mr Anthony Richards, who had been avoiding his ex-wife and her demands for child support was discovered after the wife and children arrived at a department store to see Santa Claus, only to find daddy dressed in red robes...

REMOTE EQUIPMENT

It's not often that businesses can claim legitimately to be acting in the public interest, but the good people at Wells Fargo and Mastercard could have no other reason that sheer helpfulness for installing a cashpoint machine in the McMurdo Station in Antarctica. No more than two hundred people will walk past this machine in any one year. What's more, there's not a lot of opportunity for spending cash in that corner of Antarctica. Meanwhile, a telephone company in India paid the army to install a new telephone box for them. There is nothing unusual in the installation of a telephone box, except that this one is on top of a glacier on the border with Pakistan, where temperatures regularly fall to below minus 60 degrees and wind speeds are in excess of 60 miles per hour. As if that was not bad enough, the glacier is also in the middle of a battle field, but at least the Indian army should have no trouble calling for reinforcements from now on – so long as someone remembered to bring some change.

MOTORING

We differ from almost every other creature on this planet is one vital respect: whereas the rest of the life on Earth adapted to suit its environment, we don't. We simply change our environment to suit ourselves. This means that humankind is capable of living on the sea bed, on the tops of mountains and even in space. While this has seen the development of some strikingly wonderful technology, as a species we have remained in the Stone Age, far closer to our ape ancestors than many of us would like to admit. Nowhere does this become more apparent than when we are behind the wheel of a motor car. Under these circumstances we quickly revert to form, behaving in ways that would cause us to curl up in embarrassment under any other conditions. The mild-mannered among us become raging animals, barely able to contain the desire to kill all who get in our way. The articulate are rendered dumb, and the saintly resort to language that would shock a referee. When we hit the road, the car ceases to become a triumph of modern engineering and becomes, instead, our cave on wheels. And God help anyone who dares to try and invade our space.

ROAD RUNNER

Police in Arizona were puzzled recently by a car they found crashed into the side of a cliff. It was not the crash that was causing the puzzlement, rather the fact that the car had crashed 150 feet up the side of the sheer cliff face. Closer investigation revealed that the car had been fitted with a solid-fuel rocket. A forensic report showed that in true Roadrunner fashion, the rocket had been ignited while the car was in motion, almost immediately accelerating it from around 30 mph to not less than 350 mph. The fighter-plane-like G forces would have rendered the occupant of the car unconscious for the rest of the short journey, during which the car left the road and climbed into the air, finally impacting with the cliff face. The driver was identified from fingernail fragments found embedded in what remained of the steering wheel.

CUPID STUNT

Drive-by shootings have been going on for a long time in the United States, but an incident that occurred in Brooklyn, New York, definitely had a feel of Medieval England about it. A local man was on his way home from work when he heard the screech of car tyres and shouts of abuse. Looking up, he was just in time to spot an arrow flying through the air towards him. The man was fortunate enough to be able to block the arrow with his briefcase before calling the police. So far they have failed to find the attacker, but police are said to be looking for an Englishman, about five feet seven inches tall and wearing green tights.

CANNONBALL RUN

In another case of an unusual drive-by shooting, the owner of a mobile home is having a hard time convincing his insurance company that he was the victim of an unprovoked and premeditated attack. No one is disputing that his mobile home was destroyed in the outrage, but they are having trouble finding a ballistics match for the American Civil War cannonball that was found at the scene of the crime.

TEACHING BAD HABITS

Learner drivers could be forgiven for imagining that a driving school in the US is offering lessons in road rage after one driving instructor ordered his student to "Follow that car!" The instructor was so incensed at his pupil being cut up by another driver that he got her to force the other car off the road. He then leapt from the pupil's car and attacked the other driver. After being released on $400 bail, the instructor is back at work – teaching road safety to would-be drivers.

STILL ON HOLIDAY?

A young Dutch couple made an appeal on television and radio after their caravan was stolen while they were on a journey through Spain. The couple had pulled up at a service station, where they ate lunch and rested for a while before deciding to continue on their way. There was nothing out of the ordinary about this except for the fact that the man's mother, who had died during the holiday, was being stored illegally in the caravan so that the couple could save the cost of transporting her body back to Holland by conventional means. Unfortunately, someone stole the caravan while they were having lunch. It was eventually found, but the dead mother is still missing.

THREE TIMES UNLUCKY

There are bad days and there are very bad days. One such day was suffered by Robert Monaghan, who lives in the Northern Irish town of Ballymena. While crossing the road he was hit by a small van, which drove on and left him where he lay. As he was struggling to his feet, a car hit him, this time knocking him into the gutter before driving off. A crowd of bystanders gathered to see what was going on and to wait for an ambulance to arrive. While they were waiting, a lorry reversed into the crowd, injuring three people. Fortunately, the ambulance could be heard in the distance and this time everyone stepped back to avoid being hit by the speeding vehicle – everyone except Robert Monaghan that is, who was unfortunately run over by the arriving ambulance.

HEAD TO HEAD

Two German drivers suffered a head-on collision while attempting to navigate through thick fog along the back roads of a small town. Their vehicles were, however, untouched by the incident. The accident happened because both men were driving in opposite directions, each with their head out of the window. The fog was so thick that although they managed to avoid crashing their cars into each other, they did achieve a motor-assisted mutual head-butt which resulted in cracked skulls for both of the drivers.

SORRY MUM

Parents ignore a child's warning at their peril, as a woman in Kansas discovered a little too late in life. Realizing that she was going to have difficulties backing out of her driveway, Kathy Palmer told her ten-year-old son to climb into the driving seat and reverse the car out while she guided him from the road. The boy, who could barely reach the pedals, had never driven a car forwards before let alone backwards. Despite his pleas to be allowed to remain a passenger, his mother insisted that the boy drive. Believing that he was reversing out too slowly, Mrs Palmer told her son to step on it. He did, and ran her over.

DOWN - AND OUT

A man in New York, the city that practically invented the compensation claim, was struck by a car while crossing the road. The blow was merely a glancing one as the driver had made all reasonable efforts to avoid the hapless pedestrian, who had wandered out on to the busy street without bothering to look and see if there was a car coming. Despite this, a passer-by told the man to lie down in the road and pretend that he had been badly injured on the understanding that a trip to hospital would increase his chances of an insurance payout. Unfortunately for the man, the driver of the car had been in such a hurry to check that his victim had not been badly hurt that he had jumped out of his car without putting on the handbrake. While the driver was calling an ambulance, the car rolled back and crushed the man.

BUSY BODIES

Some people just don't know when to mind their own business. The members of the Regional Airport Commission at Palm Springs in California have taken it upon themselves to issue a set of hygiene rules to the city's cab drivers, or at least those serving the airport. From now on, drivers are required to bathe regularly (remembering to use soap), to brush their teeth daily using a toothbrush and toothpaste, and are advised that the occasional use of breath-freshening mints would bring benefits to both driver and passenger. The committee stopped just short of advising the cab drivers to turn up for work in a motor car but are rumoured to be considering advising its pilots to check that they are in an aeroplane before taking off.

BUG DOCTOR

At a university in the south of England a zoology graduate is undertaking research for his publicly-funded PhD, based on the kind of insects found on windscreens after car journeys. He is concerned with creating a new system of classification for the insects based not only on the insects' type, but also the motorway on which they came to a sticky end. So, next time you see someone messing around at the front of your car, chances are he might not be putting a flyer under your wipers. It could well be that zoologist collecting the dead fliers from your windscreen.

THE JOYS OF PARENTHOOD

Anyone who suspects that rock'n'roll is not the rebellious force for change that it once was can find evidence for their argument in a story reported by *The Washington Post* after the recent gig by shock-rocker Marilyn Manson. Thousands of kids packed the arena and chanted such wholesome statements as "We hate love!" while making the sign of the Devil. Unfortunately for many of those present, the only way to get to the gig was by car. As they were too young to hold a driver's licence, they had to rely on their parents to take them to the gig. Mr Manson was kind enough to provide a waiting room for their parents – a sort of crèche in reverse – where they could sit and knit or read the paper while their little darlings had a couple of hours of rebellion time. At the end of the show, the kids trooped out, many of them wearing T-shirts emblazoned with slogans like "Kill Your Parents!", to where mummy or daddy was waiting to drive them home.

IN-CAR ENTERTAINMENT

The world is becoming an increasingly dangerous place. As stress levels rise we each become a little more impatient and minor arguments can very quickly escalate into something far worse. Take, for example, the case of a couple driving across America who got into a heated discussion about how loud the car radio should be played. He thought it was too quiet, she thought it was too loud. For nearly two hundred miles they fought and fought over control of the radio until he pulled the car over, switched off the engine, threw the keys out into the desert and set off to walk to the nearest town – a mere 12 miles away. His wife, outraged at her husband's behaviour, noted where the keys had landed, picked them up, got back into the car and set off after her husband. He turned around having assumed that she was coming to pick him up only to discover that she was driving straight at him with the intention of running him over. He survived, patched things up with his wife and together they have taken up a new hobby – target shooting.

BABY, I'M BORED...

Boredom is a terrible thing. It is not for nothing that various finger-wagging figures in history have warned that the Devil finds work for idle hands. Take, for example, the case of a man and his wife who were out driving in New Jersey at 2:00am in the morning because they had nothing better to do. When the delights of the New Jersey suburbs wore off the couple decided to light a small stick of dynamite and throw it out of the window to see what it would do. Unfortunately they failed to check to see if the window was open, before they lit the dynamite. The dynamite bounced off the window into the back of their car, where it exploded, hospitalising them both.

BRAIN DEAD

A woman in Arkansas, on her way to do her shopping, was walking from a shopping-centre car park when she noticed a woman in a car parked nearby with her hands clasped firmly behind her head and her eyes tightly shut. Assuming that the woman was asleep, she went about her business, returning to her car about 45 minutes later. The woman in the next car was in exactly the same position but with her eyes open. "Are you OK?" she shopper politely enquired. "No," came the reply, "I've been shot in the back of the head and I'm holding my brains in." Deeply alarmed, the shopper summoned the paramedics, who soon discovered that the woman in the car was in no danger at all. Apparently, a tin of bread dough had exploded on the back seat of her car, and splattered her with what she had believed to be her own brains.

BUT IT'S A BUS!

Some people just don't know when they are beaten. A bus driver in Birmingham, England, dismissed for lying on his application form, fought the case despite the overwhelming evidence against him. The driver was convicted of driving while drunk three years previously, but failed to mention this on his application form on the grounds that he had been drunk in charge of a motor car and not a bus. (As he was being employed to drive a bus and not a motor car he felt that there was no reason to mention this conviction on his application.) The reason his past caught up with him was because he raised suspicions about his competence after being found so drunk in charge of his bus that he had been unable to back it out of the depot and had fallen asleep slouched over the steering wheel.

SISTER LOVE

Kevin is not generally a name associated with obsessive, unhealthy desire. However, one major exception to this rule is Kevin O'Boyer from Oldham, near Manchester, England. He featured in news reports after the two women in his life, both of whom were pregnant by him at the time, met while travelling along in opposite directions on the M6 motorway. Pregnant girlfriend number one was heading North when she spotted the love of her life heading South with another. Spotting a break in the carriageway divide, she swung her car through 180 tyre-burning degrees and headed after them. She eventually drew level with her boyfriend's car and was horrified to discover that the other woman was, in fact, her sister – heavily pregnant by the cad.

ALL FRESHENERED UP

A man who was attempting to smuggle marijuana across a state line in America was caught after police noticed him driving erratically. They pulled him over and were instantly struck by the incredible smell coming from the man's car. Before they had even reached the driver's door, they noticed an unnaturally strong odour that seemed to be a combination of pine needles and assorted flowers. When they came to speak to the driver they realized that he was under the influence – of over a hundred air fresheners. The man had filled his car with the air fresheners in an attempt to hide the smell of the marijuana. Clearly, he had not realized that such a strong combination of evaporating chemicals would have a greater effect on him than the 10 kilos of skunk that he was carrying in the boot of his car.

DEVIL'S HIGHWAY

Residents of towns along the notorious Route 666 have been campaigning to have the name of the highway changed. Superstitious motorists are convinced that the Devil is at work on this highway, and point to the unusually high number of accidents – especially of the hit-and-run kind – that occur on this stretch of road. They say that by calling the route "666", which is, of course, The Mark Of The Beast, the authorities are inviting trouble, not least from the hordes of Satanists who regularly descend on the road to make sacrifices to Beelzebub. Some people have even claimed to see Satan behind the wheel of a large truck heading up the highway, apparently running people down for the fun of it.

ETERNAL MOTORIST

Many people form close attachments to their motor cars, but some have been known to get a little carried away. Before 71-year-old John Williams passed on, he made special preparation to make sure that he would not be separated from his beloved. Having bought 12 burial plots in a graveyard that overlooks the small Welsh village where he grew up, Mr Williams left specific instructions with his wife that he was to be buried in the seated position at the wheel of his Vauxhall Carlton. Although the local vicar was initially uneasy about performing a burial ceremony for a man and his automobile, he eventually relented and allowed the burial to go ahead. Commenting at the time, the Reverend Michael Beever said, "Although I believe that it is not possible to take one's worldly goods to heaven, I cannot help but feel that if there is a way to do it, John Wiliams will find that way."

CUTE NAME

For some deeply sad individuals, a car says more about a person than a personality ever can. Sales reps, in particular, are prone to this way of thinking, coming as they do from a world where one's success – and therefore standing as a person – is judged by the kind of car your company thinks you are worth. Some people go to extraordinary lengths in order to get their dream car and the cherry on the top of all this insane pursuit of material goods is the personalised number plate. Some people will pay a small fortune for a registration that bears even a passing resemblance to their name. Now, an English woman has gone one better. For a mere £25 – the legal fee for changing one's name – Beverley Brookes of Camden Town, London, has changed her name to C826 TBD and in doing so now has her very own personalized number plate for a fraction of the usual cost.

TREASURE TROVE

One of the biggest dangers facing motorists in Norway is the snow. Although the country is well prepared for such eventualities, skidding on snow is still a major cause of accidents in the country. So it was that in 1993 a female motorist lost her wedding ring while attempting to push her car out of a ditch after just such a skid. She imagined that the ring had been lost forever until, in 1997, she was grinding up the remains of a bull moose that her husband had shot on a hunting trip. As she was grinding the meat she noticed something shining in the bowl and found, to her immense surprise, her gold wedding ring. She believes that the ring had probably become trapped in the throat of the moose, which must have been carrying it around for almost four full years.

ARSENAL EXPERIMENTS

Police in Baltimore decided to investigate after they received a number of complaints from motorists who had become alarmed while driving along a busy road in the city. Apparently, someone had been firing two-foot long projectiles across the road with enormous speed and force. The police eventually tracked down the culprit, a 51-year-old man, who failed to see what all the fuss was about. He claimed that he was merely doing a few experiments with high explosives and had no idea that he might be inconveniencing the city's motorists in any way. In court it was revealed that it took the police over eight hours to clear the man's house of all the explosives and home-made bombs that he had accumulated.

ROAD RAGE

A driver and her daughter overreacted when a van, joining the motorway, cut them up. In anger they chased the driver for more than 12 miles down the motorway, blowing their horn and "tapping" his rear bumper with their own and, when he signalled to leave the motorway, they followed him down the slip road. At the traffic lights at the bottom of the ramp he pulled up and they stopped alongside him, "mooning" through their window. Then they turned round and headed back up the slip road they had just come down. Unfortunately, when they got to the top of the slip road they carried straight on down the motorway against the flow of traffic. They ploughed straight into an armoured security van, injuring the driver and killing themselves.

WHAT'S IN A NAME?

One thing that can be relied upon is the ability of the law and the legal system to make an ass of itself without any outside help, and some of the unusual laws in a country can be really entertaining. The United States is particularly good in this respect. While the Southern States can be relied upon to provide a rich source of silly statutes, it is often the state of California that has the truly ludicrous pieces of legislation on a subject. One bit to hit the headlines is the law regarding the use of fictitious names on driving licences. Apparently it is actually legal to use a false name on a driver's licence, even when that licence is to be used for identification purposes! The accommodating state introduced the law to help film stars get about unhindered, but now find themselves shocked to discover that some Californians are abusing that very same law with rather different motives in mind.

HATS OFF

A man in California died recently when he attempted to pick up his $10 dollar baseball cap after dropping it. Unfortunately he happened to drop it on the freeway, so he pulled his car over and unsuccessfully attempted to run across four lanes of traffic to retrieve the hat. This was almost as foolish as the weekend sailor who jumped into the deep and dangerous waters of the Mississippi River in order to retrieve his cap. He ended up drowning..

PARANORMAL

It proved to be surprisingly difficult to find stories to fill this chapter. This was not due to a lack of stories but to the nature of paranormal experiences. Every paranormal experience is, by definition, the source of a bizarre story. The difficulty was in finding paranormal experiences that were both funny and true. It is unfortunate for anyone who ever admits to such an experience that they are standing at the back of a long line of people who have a similar tale to tell. And most of the people in that queue fall into one of three categories. They are outrageous liars, simply mistaken or impossibly deluded. I find the latter are by far the most interesting group. The paranormal experience, real or not, provides a safe outlet for the attention-seeking behaviour of those who would otherwise be on the roof of a public building somewhere with a hunting rifle in their hands. By being able to claim that they have travelled to distant planets with an alien crew, these people can find the strength they need to get them through the day. On the whole, these are the people I have included in this section. Those with real paranormal experiences belong in another kind of book altogether.

KEPT IN THE DARK

This is a truly scary story and should not be read by anyone who is afraid of the dark. Two female students shared a room. One decided to go out to meet some friends, the other decided to get an early night and so asked her room-mate to turn the light off as she left. The departing student turned out the lights, but had to return an hour or so later to collect her bag. Realizing that her friend would by then be asleep, she crept into the darkened room, picked up her bag and crept out again. When she returned at the end of the evening, she found the police waiting for her. Before allowing her to enter her room the police asked her where she had been, who she had seen and what she had done that evening. Once she entered, she couldn't help but notice her friend's blood-soaked mattress and the words "Bet you're glad you didn't turn on the light" written in blood on the wall.

COMING ROUND

This tale comes from beyond the grave – well almost. A 23-year-old German woman was discovered unconscious after a drug overdose. Her parents, who discovered her, called a local doctor who pronounced her dead. Her body was taken to the mortuary where, unfortunately, one of the attendants had a taste for necrophilia. Believing the mortuary to be empty, he mounted the girl and was in mid stroke when she regained consciousness. Her screams brought help and the attendant was arrested and charged with rape. The girl's parents, however, are attempting to get the charge dropped on the grounds that their daughter would have been cremated had the attendant merely done his job.

WHICH WITCH IS WHICH?

Next time you require the services of a witch, make sure you ask to see his or her credentials first. Because of an alarming increase in the number of fake witches operating in Romania, the real witches have come together to form a union. In future, only those witches who can show a proven ability in the black arts will be admitted to the union; the rest will presumably have to join the tax office in order to commune with the undead.

HOLY RELICS

God moves in mysterious ways and who are we to question His motives in appearing to the faithful in a variety of guises, not least in the form of fruit and vegetables? In the past, the Almighty has given us the holy aubergine, the sacred tortilla and, in a break with all things vegetable, the divine duster. Now a family in Hull have been the fortunate recipients of a visitation from the all powerful and most holy one after the lady of the house, 32-year-old Linda Cole, cut open a potato while making chips and discovered a perfect cross, which had been formed from mould. The family have now erected a shrine in their freezer, where the cross can be viewed (in among the frozen peas). Rumours that the hand of God has been observed in a packet of fish fingers have so far proved unfounded.

DEAD, ALREADY

In a potentially ground-breaking case, a prisoner in Texas appealed against his death sentence on the basis that he has already died and so cannot be held accountable for crimes committed in a previous existence. The prisoner claims that because his heart stopped for nearly 90 seconds while he was undergoing a routine operation while on Death Row, he should now be viewed as having already died and therefore no longer have to face the death sentence. Prison reform groups and believers in reincarnation are eagerly awaiting the result of the appeal, especially those who claim to have been Cleopatra in an earlier incarnation and who could conceivably face charges over the death of thousands of Nubian slaves.

DEITY-FREE ZONE

Atheist Episcopalians are advertising their Sunday church services around the city of Washington, DC. Members of the group, none of whom actually believe in God or accept the notion of any kind of supreme being, joined forces out of a sense of need for some sort of community gathering on a Sunday. They have opted for a full Sunday church service minus what, for many people, is the main ingredient. When asked to explain their actions, the group's leader said: "We love the smell of incense in the morning."

ONE UP, ONE DOWN

The Friday before the funeral of Mrs Brenda Dent of Orpington, England proved to be a day of ups and down. Her family had gathered in the old lady's sitting room in order to pay their last respects. Mrs Dent's coffin lay open in the room so that the family could see her one last time before she was taken off to join the heavenly choir. As her daughter leaned over to whisper her last words to her dead mother, Mrs Dent suddenly opened her eyes and sat up. The family were delighted to discover that their loved one was not dead after all, apart, that is, from the daughter, who promptly fainted from the shock of seeing her mother return from the dead.

WITNESS FROM THE OTHER SIDE

A particularly understanding judge in Arizona allowed a very unusual witness to be called at the pre-trial hearing of a slander case. The case had been brought by Trina Kamp against a couple whom he believed had offended his church. After first dimming the lights in the courtroom, Mr Kamp went into a trance and summoned up the spirit of Dr Pahlvon Duran who, by then, had been dead for over 500 years. Not surprisingly, the spirit of Dr Duran, which was forced to communicate with the court through the body of Trina Kamp, was also deeply offended by the couple's comments and displayed a remarkable grasp of

US law. He requested that the couple be put on trial for their offensive statements.

PSYCHIC SPRING-CLEAN

New Yorkers are second only to the residents of Los Angeles in their desire to embrace what has come to be termed "New Age Culture". So keen are they to pursue a lifestyle based on the album covers of progressive rock bands from the Seventies, that the city is now awash with people offering various psychic services. The latest of these, according to *Elle* magazine, is one Julienne Kopecny, who offers a house cleaning service with a difference. For between $300 and $2,500, she will come around to your house or flat and cleanse it of any evil auras, restoring the balance of psychic powers as she goes. She specializes in cleaning up the spiritual mess left by the dead, but is also prepared to remove any traces of bad feelings left over after arguments.

MY LITTLE VOODOO

Anyone thinking of picking a fight with a neighbour in Tokyo had better think twice as a company there has just released a brand new means of revenge on to the market. Called the "Curse Kit", it is designed to allow someone to attack an enemy by harnessing the power of the dark forces. The kit comes complete with a victim look-a-like straw doll, a bag of nails (to push through the doll), a manual of tried and tested curses, and, as a special introductory offer, an effigy designed to ward off any counter-curses. The manufacturers believe they are on to a winner and look forward to selling the kit to the victims of hellish neighbours, bullied children and, most disturbingly of all, those who have lost in love.

ALIEN AERODROME

Should UFOs ever decide to land in Brazil they will encounter no such problems with finding an audience. Brazil is known as a "hot spot" among UFO enthusiasts because of the number of flying saucers that have been sighted in the skies over that country and now the Brazilian government is going out of its way to make any alien tourist welcome. They plan to be the first country in the world to build a landing site for flying saucers and have begun work on the project at Barra da Gracas in the Pantanal region of the country. The man who dreamt up the scheme, Valdon Vardac, claims that he is doing the whole of humanity a service.

ELECTRICAL APPARITION

A couple in Wales came up with one of the most unusual reasons ever for refusing to pay their electricity bills. Having run up a staggering bill of £3,000 for a single quarter's worth of electricity, the couple – George and Erma Henge, both 47 years of age – stated that they would not pay for the power used, claiming that the electricity was being consumed by an evil presence that had taken over their home. In support of their argument, they produced a freelance exorcist, a Mr Philip Marks who lived close to them. Mr Marks stated that the Henges were not responsible for the electricity that had been used and even went so far as to suggest that the electricity board should pay the bill for his professional services rather than Mr and Mrs Henge. The electricity board was so impressed by his evidence that they cut the Henge's supply off within a week of receiving his report.

GHOST IN THE MACHINE

Do computers have souls? Many people talk to their computers and more than a few of us have even had the occasional cross word, but a company in Manchester acquired a computer that attempted to talk back. Having bought the machine, they were very disappointed to find that it did not carry out the instructions it was given. On several occasions it went back to the manufacturer but no fault could be found. Initially, the problem had been that the computer displayed strange rune-like characters or would simply turn itself off for no good reason. Eventually, staff in the office where it was kept unplugged the computer and left it in a corner where it was supposed to stand until the manufacturer came to pick it up and take it away for good. Then things got really strange. Despite being unplugged, the screen began to flash brightly and ghostly moans were heard to emerge from within the equipment. In the end, staff refused to go into the office until the computer was taken away and an exorcism had been carried out.

SHOOT'EM'UP

In what can only be described as a very strange case of Southern Manners – as such behaviour is known in the States – an elderly man was found shooting at the sky above his own house with a shotgun. It seems that while relaxing on his back porch and knocking back a few beers, the old man spotted a group of UFOs approaching his house in close formation. At this point he reached for his shotgun, deciding to have a real-life game of Space Invaders. He fired so many shots that he not only succeeded in driving away the alien menace, but also attracted the attention of the local sheriff. When interviewed later, the sheriff indicated that there may have been some truth in the man's claims but added that this behaviour had lent new meaning to the words: "you ain't from round these parts, boy?"

POISONOUS IN DEATH

When 31-year-old Diamanda Lunt met her end, she left behind an unusual legacy. Staff at the hospital where she died noticed a disturbing smell coming from her body shortly after she passed on. The very first nurse who commented on the smell promptly keeled over. Her colleagues were unable to revive her and she spent two weeks in intensive care. The authorities were alerted and an autopsy was ordered. Wearing biohazard suits, pathologists cut into the body and watched as every warning system in the room went off. For some reason the body was producing enormous quantities of poisonous fumes and despite their best efforts, the pathologists were unable to find a cause for this perplexing phenomenon.

DEADLY DIGITS

Many people are aware of what has come to be known in some quarters as Desert Disease – an affliction affecting certain young men who, in the presence of someone to whom they are attracted, suddenly develop wandering palms. The condition has now been recognized by members of the medical profession, who refer to it as Alien Hand Syndrome. This condition was first recognized by the German neurologist Kurt Goldstein, who recorded a case in 1908 of a woman who was afraid to go to sleep for fear that her left hand would attack her while she slept. In a test case in America recently, one man applied through the courts to have his left hand removed by doctors on the grounds that it was a danger to his person. Despite accepting that the man was perfectly sane and rational and also recognizing that he was suffering from a distressing medical condition, the court refused his application.

REMOTE CONTROL

Ever since the Fifties, both the CIA and the KGB have been investigating the claims made by certain people that they can travel through space and time and make accurate observations using a technique known as remote viewing. While the military advantages this technique would offer for any country that could develop it are obvious, the big problem has been finding people who can do it to order. When put on the spot and asked to investigate the contents of, for example, a locked safe, no remote viewer has been able to deliver the goods. It may be the case, however, that remote viewing was never intended for anything as mundane as military purposes. Some of the more interesting claims of the remote viewers include those of having spoken to Jesus and the very firm conviction that the New Mexico desert is populated by Martians.

PATENT NONSENSE

Successful people always attract lunatics; where there's a large fortune there's usually a deranged person or two. Sometimes, however, there can appear to be a point to their madness. Bill Gates, who is rapidly becoming known as Billionaire Bill, has seen his fortune grow to one of the largest in the world, and his Microsoft Corporation has products in almost every home and office that contains a computer. Some claim that this degree of world domination is not due to Microsoft's aggressive marketing strategies that have led to virtual monopoly, but to Bill Gates's links with the Devil. Indeed, some go so far as to claim that the Gates is actually the Devil incarnate, sent to Earth to destroy civilization. As evidence for this they point out that when Mr Gates's full name is spelt out in ASCII (American Standard Code for Information Interchange, used to represent alphabetical characters numerically) with a bit of deft manipulation and adding up, it's possible to derive the figure 666, the number traditionally associate with the Devil.

PLUMBING THE DEPTHS

We've all heard of haunted castles, houses, theatres and even ships, but how many people can claim to have a haunted toilet? English magazine *The Big Issue* published the story of a man in New York who claimed that his toilet was haunted by the ghost of a missing plumber. The plumber disappeared while on the job and was never seen again. The last known sighting of him was several years ago at the New Yorker's apartment. The plumber went there to fix a leaking toilet many years previously, but never returned. The man claims that the toilet is haunted, and even tried to pull him in one night – a battle that resulted in him suffering a broken pelvis. Despite this, the owner continues to use the toilet and has even become used to the sound of the cistern whispering the plumber's name in the dead of night.

DEVILISH DESIRES

Two inmates of the notorious Louisiana State Penitentiary are currently taking legal action against the prison, its governor and the state of Louisiana. The men claim that they are not being allowed to pursue their religion of choice – Satanism. They are demanding equal access to the prison chapel and have also requested that the state provides them with the usual paraphernalia of Devil worship – black capes and candles, daggers and a sacrificial virgin. The men, who are serving life sentences for murder, rape and robbery, claim that by being denied access to these things, they are also being denied the chance for eternal salvation in the arms of Satan. A spokesman for the prison authorities expressed regret but added that he felt that their behaviour in this world had already guaranteed their final destination in the next.

PUSSY PATROL

Every national security service is a product of the country in which it developed. British intelligence is notorious for being staffed by legions of well-connected, nice-but-dim types. By contrast, the CIA tends to be staffed by people whose grades were not quite good enough to get into the Harvard Business School. Low-grade recruits can be the only possible explanation for an experiment carried out by the CIA in the Sixties, when they fitted a cat with a listening device and trained it to follow enemy agents. Cats do not take well to this kind of training and so the process took a number of years. All went well to start with and the agents were able to hear the conversations of the man the cat was following. However, a problem arose when their man decided to cross a busy road. Listening from two blocks away, the last sounds the agents heard from the cat's transmitter was a screech of brakes.

FOOTBALL MAGIC

The run-up to a football World Cup competition is always an exciting time for fans of the game. A little-known story that emerged during preparations for one World Cup competition involved a game between Peru and Colombia. Lacking true faith in his country's team's ability to win the match, Peruvian medicine man Juan Oscora tried to use a little black magic to give his side an advantage. Having first made voodoo dolls representing the Colombian team, he ritually burned, tortured and dismembered them. He said that he did this in order to drain their energy, destroy their team spirit and thereby cause them to lose the match. Despite following the rites of the ritual to the letter, Juan Oscora's efforts came to little as his side ended up just about managing a draw with the mighty Colombians.

FISHY FELLOW

This story has ended up in the paranormal section of this book, although it really belongs in a section of its own, which could be labelled abnormal. It concerns the death of one Neil Watson, a 49-year-old Australian from the town of Toolondo. When police found his body he was dressed in a rubber wet suit that had been altered to resemble the shape of a fish. Mr Watson, described as a nice man who occasionally got into trouble after he forgot to take his medicine, had a history of trying to emulate fish. One theory of his death is that he was trying to hop to a pond at the bottom of his garden while wearing the wet suit, but the Australian heat, combined with the complete lack of oxygen in the all-in-one suit, caused him to collapse from exhaustion. Police have dismissed claims that he was performing a bizarre ritual which would have led to him being reincarnated as a fish.

MYSTIC MANIFESTO

As the millennium approaches, one British political party has already begun its preparations for the next General Election. The Alien Visitors' Party, led by Mystic Merlin (George Vernon to his mum), has already produced a manifesto, even though it is far from being a mainstream party. Mystic Merlin claims that he has been specially selected by the aliens to represent their interests during their time on Earth. To this end he plans to ensure that, when his party triumphs in the next election, it will be sure to outlaw all couch potatoes, ban all weapons, teach common sense, and make organic food a compulsory component of everyone's diet. When questioned about the party's stance on education and the reorganization of the National Health Service, Mr Vernon responded by saying that these issues were a matter for the aliens themselves, but added that he expected the Health Service to be safe in their hands.

FIRESTARTER

Yet another tale from the "it wasn't me" school of crime emerges from the Wirral, near Liverpool, England. A man who was arrested and charged with arson had a thoroughly plausible explanation for what had happened. When questioned at some length about the fire the man, 29-year-old Paul Smith, stated that he was not guilty of starting the fire but did concede that the fire may well have started because he had willed it to do so. Apparently, fires start around him whenever he "wills" it to happen, and have done so ever since he was a young child. Despite this, the police charged him with arson anyway – on the grounds that his finger prints were found on a can of paraffin found near the scene of the crime.

ORIGAMI WITH A DIFFERENCE

An extraordinarily enterprising shopkeeper in Hong Kong is doing a roaring trade in paper copies of everyday objects. For a certain fee, the man is prepared to sell paper cell-phones, paper computers and even full-sized paper motor cars. The people who buy these items do so in order to burn them in Chinese ceremonies which are carried out to honour the dead. Apparently the Chinese believe that even in the hereafter it is important to display one's wealth; the paper consumer goods go up in flames in order that they might reach the intended recipient in Heaven.

SINGING IN THE RAIN

One of the interesting things about writing a book like this is discovering that there is a whole world of career opportunities that were never discussed in school. Where, for example, was the careers advice on the job of Freelance Bigfoot Hunter? Not that this was a problem for a gentleman in the Northwest Territories of Canada. The intrepid hunter set off in pursuit of the fearsome beast one day in November and ended up having to camp in the forest for the night. All went well until he was disturbed in the night by what he later described as a trickling sound. In a state of blind panic at the prospect of being eaten by the beast, he fired off a distress flare. This prompted the rescue service to fly all the way out from Toronto to rescue him from the rain. The cost to the tax payer? A mere $8,500.

POSSESSED

American courts are in danger of being overrun by nuisance law suits undertaken by "no win, no fee" lawyers. An example of this kind of law suit, one which elevates the merely legal to the level of an art form, was filed in Washington against a Roman Catholic archbishop. A Mr Anthony Richards sought, claiming that the church was responsible for him becoming possessed by the Devil. Mr Richards claims that it was as a result of this possession that he dropped out of college, took up smoking cigarettes, began speaking in tongues, and developed a fascination for homosexual acts, although he strenuously denied every taking part in any. He sought $100 million in damages, but claimed to be willing to settle out of court if the archbishop performed an exorcism upon him.

THE LIVING DEAD

An Argentinean man, who glories in the name of Robinson Gonzalez, shocked mourners at his funeral by banging on the door of the chapel of rest and demanding to be let in. His mother suffered an anxiety attack when presented with the sight of her son walking around among the mourners and had to be taken outside for some air. Fortunately, she made a complete recovery and considered the whole experience to be God's way of testing her. Apparently she had identified a body, in the police morgue, as her son, however, it turned out that she hadn't had a proper look on the grounds that she did not wish to remember her darling son with gunshot wounds.

POLITICS

There is very little politicians can do that is not, by the very nature of the way they have chosen to lead their lives, bizarre. These are the people who can tell the kind of lies that would make a barrister blush and yet continue to claim to speak for all of us, despite the obvious animosity at least half the population probably feels toward them at any one time. The truth of the matter is that with very few exceptions, politicians are simply the very annoying people who come round every few years and ask us to vote for them in the very costly and ultimately pointless popularity contest that is the modern election. There was a time when leaders appointed themselves. They were not kind people, they were strong people who inspired a combination of respect and fear in all who met them. Today we are presented with a dreary combination of failed lawyers and unimaginative, self-serving businessmen and invited to take our pick. Under these circumstances I always take Billy Connolly's advice: "If you wouldn't drink with the man, don't vote for him." This section is dedicated to those few brave souls who have, in the past, treated politicians with the degree of respect they deserve.

UNDER THE MOON

A man in Vienna, charged with showing his butt to the German Chancellor Helmut Kohl, appealed against his sentence on the grounds that Herr Kohl could not have seen his bottom from where he was standing at the time of the incident. In order to prove his case, he wanted to appear on an identity parade (with nine others) and challenge the Chancellor to pick his bottom out from among the other "Mooners".

ATTENTION TO DETAIL

Democracy in action is a wonderful thing to observe. Take the example of Tim Moor, who sponsored a resolution through the Texas House Of Representatives calling for the assembly to recognise the unique work of Albert de Salvo, pointing out that the state of Massachusetts had already taken note of his "unconventional techniques involving population control and applied psychology". The resolution was, of course, passed unanimously. Mr Moor had presented the bill in order to demonstrate the care and attention most of his fellow representatives apply to their work. Albert de Salvo is better known as the Boston Strangler.

DEAD BUT NOT GONE

A magnificent example of the power of The People is provided by a case which came before the Oklahoma Supreme Court in December 1990. Josh Evans, who is a lawyer (like so many of the unsavoury characters who run for political office), claimed victory over the incumbent, Frank Ogden III, despite polling only nine per cent of the vote. He had assumed that being an able lawyer and a living person gave him an advantage over the winner, who had polled 91 per cent of the vote despite the fact that he had died three months before the election.

PICKY PICKY

The minds of some jobsworths leaves a lot to be desired. I've no doubt that the official who turned down a federal grant application for research into technology for the disabled – because the application form had not been typed with double spacing – had his own good reasons. But I wonder about the Georgia Court of Appeal. The court turned down – without leave to appeal – an appeal by the state itself against a personal injury compensation pay out. The appeal had been typed using the New Times Roman typeface rather than the Courier typeface which should have been used for legal jargon.

DEADLY CONCLUSION

According to US government statistics, people who keep guns at home are nearly three times more likely to be murdered, usually by someone they know. Interestingly enough, very few gun owners are ever able to protect their lives or property with their weapons, but tend instead to cause an intruder to take drastic action against them. When these statistics were put to the National Rifle Association, a political organization established to protect the constitutional right of Americans to bear arms, no matter what their IQs, they were dismissed out of hand. When asked why, a spokesman claimed that the statistics were inaccurate on the grounds that murdered gun owners: "were highly susceptible to homicide. We know that because they were killed."

BROTHERS IN OUTLAW

While the politicians struggle to find a peaceful solution to the Arab-Israeli conflict, it would seem that peace has already broken out among certain sections of both communities. Car thieves on both sides of the divide have decided to bury their differences in the name of profit, giving Israel the largest per-capita car theft problem in the world and proving that Israeli-Palestinian car-theft rings can succeed where politicians fail.

BANNED BY THE KLAN

Karen Carter, who is the head of a branch of the National Association for the Advancement of White People is clearly someone who has little time for details or small print. A Pittsburgh newspaper has reported that her application to join the Ku Klux Klan was turned down after Klan members impressed with her work met with her to discuss the possibility of closer co-operation between the two groups. The Klan, which has a long tradition of accepting every kind of white trash, felt compelled to reject her application – on the grounds that she is a black, single mother.

DRUNK IN CHARGE

The chairperson of a North of England council's alcohol and drug abuse committee found herself in hot water when she was arrested for drink driving after a council workers' Christmas party. Despite being found to be nearly three times over the legal drink-driving limit, the woman insisted that she would not be resigning from the committee. In a statement that would seem to indicate that she might well have a wonderful future in politics, the chairperson said: "My knowledge has now been broadened considerably by this experience and I believe that it will allow me to bring a new dimension to my work, enabling me to become an even more effective member of the committee."

CHEW ON THAT!

A voter in the American city of Oregon expressed his views on the local mayor in a way that might well appeal to any number of people who feel that politicians only take note of their constituents during election times. The man, who has yet to be identified and therefore rightly hailed as the hero he undoubtedly is, walked up to the mayor and, without bothering to say a word, vomited all over the elected representative. The mayor was, for once, stunned into silence – so much so, that he failed to call for help and the man was able simply to walk out of the council chamber and go about his business of righting wrongs and making the world safe for democracy.

FAMINE RELIEF

The people of North Korea have been able to take great comfort, despite a national famine, from the promotion of the head of their communist party, Kim Jong Il. He had held the relatively junior post of "Dear Leader", but has been promoted to that of "Great Leader". This, claimed the government, was cause for jubilation and was definitely reason enough for the people to stop complaining about the obvious lack of food in their country. The government has even gone so far as to point out that Mother Nature herself has come over all funny at the news.

COMBAT FLOWERS

A battle has erupted within the ranks of the American Army. Having run out of easy targets in the Third World and in the Middle East, the military are now picking fights with each other. Things have become so bad that two generals have even become involved. The cause of the punch up? The right to sell flowers. It seems that the branch of the military that sells foodstuffs on military bases has started to sell garden plants. This so offended the base exchanges (the military equivalent of department stores), who believed that they had the exclusive rights to sell flowers, that they have now begun to sell large amounts of food at a discounted price in order to drive the food shops out of business. According to the *New York Times*, a spokesman for the army has admitted that "This is war".

DRUNK BY DICTATORS

A family-run wine business in Italy is facing pressure from consumer groups and refugee organisations to do something about its marketing. The wine producers are being asked to change the names of their best-selling wines in order to avoid annoying certain sections of the community. Despite their earlier flirtations with fascism, many Italians are offended by two varieties of wine which feature a picture of Adolf Hitler on the label and are called Zieg Heil and Ein Volk, Ein Reich, Ein Fuehrer (One People, One Empire, One Ruler). The company believes that it would not be right to remove these particular brands while demand for their Lenin and Marx brands continues to decline.

JUDGE JUDGED

After imprisoning a couple for non-payment of taxes, a judge in Kansas has been impeached by a radical-patriot jury (the kind that feels that most Americans came to America to get away from the kind of people who now run America). In a truly wonderful example of the power of the people under the US constitution, the judge was accused of kidnapping (for jailing the couple), of going against the peoples' God-given right to own land (especially the bits previously owned by troublesome natives) and of helping to defend a racketeering conspiracy (the US tax service). Also added to his list of crimes was the fact that he failed to display the US flag in his courtroom and allowed his clerk to sign documents in the middle of the dotted line rather than to the left. God Bless America!

JEWISH JOKE

The right to pursue one's religious beliefs without fear or prejudice is protected by the laws of most civilised countries. In the United States, the right to free worship (of God) is even enshrined in the constitution, which makes it seem all the more surprising that a judge in Iowa should refuse these basic human rights to two inmates of the state prison who wished to participate in Jewish ceremonies. However, when asked to justify his decision, the judge was able to argue with some conviction that he took the decision based on the grounds that the prisoners were not Jewish, knew less about Judaism than most gentiles, and were probably interested only in getting their hands on ceremonial fruits and shawls. Apparently, it is not uncommon for prisoners to use the fruits to make wine and the shawls to strangle other prisoners.

GRAVE MISTAKE

A tribe of Native Americans in Kansas earned the displeasure of the council of Kansas City and four other tribes after they announced plans to build a casino on the site of an ancient burial ground. The tribe planned to erect the gambling den despite countless warnings of the unspeakable horrors that await anyone who violates sacred ground, or as one protester put it: "I don't think my great-grandfather would wish to spend eternity looking up at a lot of old ladies playing cards."

APPROPRIATE PUNISHMENT

As John Mortimer (a man who describes himself as the best writer to have ever defended a murderer) once pointed out, the trouble with any legal system is that no-one ever sets out to commit a crime in the sure and certain knowledge that they will be caught and punished for it. However, the justice department in Malaysia seems to have turned this idea on its head with a new directive to the country's prison governors. Apparently, from now on, anyone convicted of "sexual deviancy" will receive not only a prison sentence, but can also expect to be bound and whipped into the bargain. It is believed that a group of British MPs have expressed an interest in studying this approach to crime and punishment and have even offered to pay their own fares over to Malaysia.

JUDGE DUDE

If you ever end up in court, you should hope that it is in front of a judge like Ralph H Baldwin. Ralph was forced to resign from his job after only three months when a petty-minded court clerk accused him of being a little over familiar with jurors and lawyers in his court. According to the kill-joy, at the end of one case the judge invited two jurors and a defence lawyer back into the jury room where they worked their way through a crate of beers and put the world to rights.

TRANSFERRING THE BLAME

British supporters of the "no win, no fee" system for lawyers should look to the American courts before giving the idea their full backing. Because clients can sue without worrying about the cost of losing, some very usual cases come before the courts. For instance, a Wisconsin man sued the state authorities because they paid him his disability allowance in a lump sum. He spent most of the money in a week (on wine, women, song and gambling) before wasting the rest on living expenses. He claims that the fact that the money is now all gone is the fault of the government who should have given the money to him as a weekly allowance. In a statement to reporters the man said: "It's their fault. Giving me that money was like putting a gun to my head and saying shoot yourself."

NAILING UP DEMANDS

Anyone who has any doubts about the quality of the drugs being produced in Columbia should look to the case of three factory workers who decided to stage a protest at plans to reorganise their work place – a reorganisation that would have caused large-scale job losses. Not content with staging sit-ins or threatening all-out strike action, the men decided to take the less obvious route to a successful strike – they had themselves crucified. The men erected crosses on common land opposite the factory and then got friends to hammer 5 inch nails through their hands to hold them into place. After 50 wincing hours on their crosses, the management of the factory eventually agreed to the workers' demands.

TAXING THOUGHTS

There is more than a little truth to the statement: "Just because he's in charge doesn't mean he knows what he's doing." A similar thought must have passed through the minds of the unfortunate citizens of Morris, Alabama after the Inland Revenue Service seized the city's assets for none payment of taxes. In the end, any awkwardness that might have existed between these rival tools of government were resolved when the IRS mortgaged the City Hall, thereby raising the necessary monies to pay the town's tax bill.

LITTLE RAMBOS

The right to bear arms that is entrenched in the American constitution, is causing problems in a number of schools. A junior-school-aged child in California was recently suspended from all classes after he turned up carrying bags of home-made napalm that he had made using a formula he found on the Internet. The problem in parts of Illinois, however, has become so bad that police are now offering special inducements to children in an effort to get them to hand over their weapons. As part of a "Guns For Toys" campaign, police are swapping cuddly toys for guns and knives that children hand over.

THE OLDEST PROFESSION

A candidate for the job of mayor of a small town in Virginia went on television to explain his actions after he was arrested for seeking the services of a prostitute. He explained that he had always been in favour of legalizing prostitution and also that he had sought out these women, not so much for their sexual services, as for the fact that they didn't judge him on his looks. In a similar not-quite-getting-the-point story, a priest in Kentucky was criticized after he vigorously defended a murderer from the pulpit on the grounds that, although the man had killed large number of people, he was not an atheist – which, in his eyes, was a far greater crime.

EDIBLE UNDERWEAR

A city council member in Houston, Texas, clearly felt that there was so little crime in his city that he could spend time harassing the owners of a shop called Condoms & More. He managed to persuaded the local sheriff's department to send the vice squad in on a raid on the shop but was bitterly disappointed when they were unable to find any evidence of even the slightest bit of criminal activity. Undeterred, he then approached the city's public health department who did their bit to protect the community by ordering the shop to dispose of such items as edible panties and breast-shaped chocolate lollipops. The owners of the shop reluctantly disposed of the offending items thus enabling the good citizens of Houston to sleep in their beds at night safe in the knowledge that no one was attempting to sell edible underwear without a licence.

TAXING THOUGHTS

There is more than a little truth to the statement: "Just because he's in charge doesn't mean he knows what he's doing." A similar thought must have passed through the minds of the unfortunate citizens of Morris, Alabama after the Inland Revenue Service seized the city's assets for none payment of taxes. In the end, any awkwardness that might have existed between these rival tools of government were resolved when the IRS mortgaged the City Hall, thereby raising the necessary monies to pay the town's tax bill.

WELL GOTTEN GAINS

If anyone harbours doubts as to the good intentions of politicians, they should look at the example of two Missouri State Legislators who proposed, what they described as, a bill to promote good, clean family life in the southern state. The bill attempted to reward the clean living with a sum of $1,000. In return for this money, married couples would have to prove that they were over the age of 21, did not have any sexually transmitted diseases, did not produce any children outside of wedlock, had never gone through with an abortion, and have never got a divorce from an earlier partner. These conditions were put on the deal in an effort to promote, what the policy makers called, the Missouri code of Chastity and Faithfulness.

SEX

Sex was always going to be a difficult subject for a good Catholic boy like me to deal with. Somewhere at the back of my mind was the thought that my mother was going to read this, or even worse, my priest. What follows is not, in any sense, prurient. Rather, it serves mostly to highlight the fallibility of humans everywhere. Most of us indulge in sex at some time in our lives – some do little else. It is the most basic of desires and can sometimes even surpass that of the desire for food. To condemn it is to deny our very nature and is the very height of foolishness. What follows are amusing tales of people who seem, somehow, to have lost the plot. Whether it is at the hands of the Church or some other corrupting influence, these people have forgotten that sex is supposed to be fun. Enjoy the consequences.

...BUT NOT SHEEP

A Welsh man sued a hypnotist who placed him in a trance during a show at his local bar. The man claims that his life was ruined after the hypnotist told him to make love to a chair on the stage. The man testified in court that ever since this night he has remained in the grip of the hypnotic spell and is unable to escape from it. As a result, the man has attempted to simulate sex with his mattress, his washing machine, tumble drier, every chair in the house and even his bath.

MAKING THE BREAST OF IT

The Inland Revenue Service has never had a sense of humour when it comes to claiming legitimate expenses against tax. For some reason, tax assessors assume that everyone is out to pay as little tax as possible and as a result, tax officers object to many very reasonable claims for tax reductions. One such objection came before the US Tax Court after an exotic dancer named Cynthia S Hess, who works under the name "Chesty Love", claimed a rebate of over $2,000 for depreciation on the cost of her breast implants, which had enlarged her bust to an unlikely 56FF. The court upheld her claim on the grounds that her breasts were sufficiently cumbersome as to make her appear "freakish" and therefore she could not possibly be said to derive personal benefit from them.

A LOAD OF BULL

Afghan tribesmen are seldom in any hurry to get married. This may have something to do with a beverage that is traditionally drunk on the wedding night. This delightful brew is called Khoona and is thought to be a very potent aphrodisiac. Quite why anyone would wish to indulge their sexual desires after drinking it is a mystery to many people, however, as the brew consists mostly of still-warm, very recently acquired bull's semen.

...AND NOW THE NUDES

Cable television subscribers in Washington were treated to a night of unremitting hardcore pornography after computers belonging to the local cable operator went haywire and sent ten hours of nakedness and humping down the system. These adult movies would normally go out on pay-per-view channels only, but the computer error resulted in all viewers receiving them, regardless of personal tastes, subscription status or their views on such programming. What is perhaps most interesting about the whole matter is that the cable station received only 11 complaints about the films – from people who were worried that they might have to pay for the unrequested service.

PUBLIC CONFESSION

Nearly all local radio stations seem to employ at least one DJ who is out to make a name for himself by amusing his listeners with prank calls. One such DJ in Texas opened a can of worms when he called a woman live on air and informed her that her husband had been fired for "unprofessional conduct" after sleeping with a number of his junior colleagues. The woman was annoyed at first, but then found the silver lining in an otherwise very dark cloud. "Oh, well," she announced live on air to the entire state, "I suppose this means that I don't have to feel guilty about my affair with his brother."

LAY PREACHER

The sheriff of a small town in Kansas was always giving the locals grief about their moral standards, even going so far as to denounce them from the pulpit on a Sunday in his capacity as lay-preacher of the town church. Imagine the locals delight then, when the sheriff returned a rented video to his video shop having accidentally left a tape in the box of himself and his good wife dressed in bondage gear and going at it for a good hour and a half. Within a week, more than 500 copies of the tape were circulating around the town, and the man himself was nowhere to be seen.

JELLY BABY

In the latest in a long line of nuisance lawsuits, a woman in America sued her local chemist after she was sold a jar of contraceptive jelly. The woman was most disturbed to find that, despite the fact that she spread the jelly on her toast every morning, she still somehow managed to get pregnant. Her lawyers are claiming that she was conned out of the price of the contraceptive jelly, which costs a great deal more than ordinary jam, and that she had bought it in good faith believing it to be an edible contraceptive. The woman is demanding half a million dollars for the inconvenience she will have to endure.

DOGGY STYLE

Few of us will ever have to endure the embarrassment suffered by a legal secretary in Birmingham, England recently. Her colleagues decided to hold a surprise party for her at her home. All day long they kept quiet about the party, before sneaking off early and leaving her with an enormous amount of work to finish before she could leave for home. In the meantime, they entered her house using her spare keys and waited for her, along with her dog, in the living room. Unfortunately, our secretary headed straight for the kitchen on arriving home. After a while she burst into the living room in search of her pet. Alas, while in the kitchen she had stripped naked and covered her genitals in peanut butter before going in search of her dog.

NEVER MIND THE SMELL

A Parisian found himself in court after his neighbours resorted to complaining to the police about the terrible smell that was coming from his apartment. Despite the protests of his neighbours, the man refused to do anything about the smell and as the days went by it began to get unbearable. When the police called round to find out what was happening they were met with abuse and the man refused them entry into his flat. Smelling a rat, or something worse, they went away and got a search warrant. On their return, they found that the man had dug up his recently-deceased girlfriend and had been having sex with what remained of her body.

HORIZONTAL ADVOCACY

A woman who made a career out of law (the world's second-oldest profession) was dismissed from the prestigious Chicago-based law firm she had been working for. The reason? She had been convicted too many times for practising the world's oldest profession. Dismissing her after her most recent conviction for prostitution, the firm issued a statement saying that it would not tolerate the presence of a prostitute within its ranks. Insiders believe that the real reason she was dismissed was because jealous colleagues were outraged at the fact that she made even more money on her back than they did in court.

BREAST INTENTIONS

A man in Chicago has filed a lawsuit against the owners of a strip club in the city and also against a stripper with the highly plausible name of Lusty Busty. The man, who is demanding more than $100,000, claims that he has had to wear a neck brace ever since one fateful night when he entered the club and was given a front row seat. He claims that Miss Busty deliberately battered him around the head and neck with her breasts, thereby causing the damage. Lusty, and the club's owners, are preparing to call nearly 60 men to the stand who are prepared to swear, under oath, that their lives have not been in any way altered for the worse by the experience of having been on the receiving end of Miss Lusty's 64FF breasts.

GHOULISH GRAN

It's not unheard of for mothers to try and find a nice girl for their son, even if it means going to extremes, in their ultimate quest for the all-important grandchild. However, one elderly mother in Milwaukee is proving to be more determined than most. The average mother would accept the death of her son as the end of any hopes of grandchildren, but not this one. She advertised for a surrogate mother to use her dead son's sperm and offered to pay large sums of money to anyone of childbearing age willing to help her to fulfil her ambition of becoming a grandmother. The advertisement didn't explain how mummy had got hold of the sperm.

BRING YOUR VIAGRA!

The National Sexual Rights Council, a pressure group formed by and on behalf of prostitutes, has been hard at work raising funds in California with the aim of getting underage girls off the streets in red light districts of cities including Los Angeles and San Francisco. Just like an ordinary church bazaar, the women have been setting out stalls and selling T-shirts, badges and mugs emblazoned with the group's logo. And just like the average church bazaar, they have been selling raffle tickets. Most of the prizes consist of said T-shirts, badges and mugs, but the first prize, which they claim is worth over $150,000, consists of a night at the famous Rooster Shack in Nevada, one of the few licensed brothels in America.

THREE FATHERS, ONE SON

One young boy found himself the subject of a legal battle after two men each petitioned the court for custody. The child's mother had convinced each of the men, separately, that he was the child's father. She also told each man that she did not wish to live with him. Neither man knew of the other's existence and both seemed prepared to put up with the situation. All went well until the mother became confused over whose turn it was to visit the child. Both men arrived at the same time and both went away swearing that he would get custody of his son. To this end, they both took blood tests – which proved to the court that neither man is the boy's father.

WHIPPED CREAM

Very few major cities are free of pretentious theme restaurants, and New York is certainly no exception. La Lash, an addition to this sorry group of eateries, is offering a twist on the theme idea. In return for parting with enormous sums of money, diners can enjoy the delights of S&M while they eat food served to them in dog bowls. Waiters and waitresses can be persuaded to administer beatings to slow eaters and will even reward those who leave a large tip with the opportunity to beat their fellow diners. Why anyone would wish to go to such a place remains a mystery, particularly to anyone who went to a British Catholic school in the 1970s, where such behaviour was commonplace and where the food was an awful lot cheaper.

METER MAID

The English are almost universally mocked, albeit affectionately, for their reserve, which at times reaches almost Vulcan proportions – it has been said that the English are always two drinks behind the rest of the world. A classic illustration of this legendary reserve can be seen in a case reported in Britain's Sunday Express. For reasons too dull to explain, a housewife was standing naked in her own kitchen (no longer a criminal offence in the UK) when she heard the baker's delivery van arrive.

Fearing that the baker would see her, she dived into a cupboard. There was a knock at the door, to which she replied "Come in", believing that the baker would leave the bread on the table before going on his way. To her horror, she heard footsteps approaching the cupboard door. The gas man opened the door, spied the naked woman and explained that he had come to read her meter. "Oh. I'm sorry," she said "I was expecting the baker." Saying nothing, the gas man nodded sagely and excused himself.

MIGHTY MAMMARIES

Japanese television continues in it efforts to reach new lows with the introduction of a show in which, for no good reason, young women clad only in skimpy bikinis entertain the viewing public by crushing aluminium drinks cans between their breasts. Certainly, this is a novel way of reminding the public of the importance of recycling, but maybe it is simply a ratings booster – who can say?

FAST FOOD, FAST FILTH

These days it is not unusual to find that the person asking you if you would "like fries with that" has got a university degree. As the job market shrinks and the number of graduates rises it is inevitable that there will be a shift in patterns of graduate employment. In some countries, however, the situation is already serious. *The Economist* magazine recently reported on the job situation in Cuba, and made special mention of a highly qualified engineer who spends his days selling pork sandwiches on street corners. However, his life is not as bad as it might seem – he takes the profits from his sandwich business and ploughs them back into pornographic videos, which he shows at select gatherings of farmers and their wives for five pesos per head. So popular are the screenings that the country folk clamour to see the same films over and over again – for a repeat fee, of course.

SCHOOLGIRL SMUT

The *New York Times* reported from Japan about a very worrying trend among certain sections of the community. Apparently Japan's business warriors are becoming increasingly fascinated with very young girls, and a whole host of magazines has sprung up to cater to their tastes. Hiroyuki Fukuda, the editor of a magazine with the frankly disturbing title of *Anatomical Illustrations Of Young*

Girls, was questioned at length about this development. He justified his magazine on the grounds that it did not cater for the real perverts, who, as he so thoughtfully pointed out, are only really interested in the under tens – although he was willing to concede that the age of the girls that his readership finds most interesting is falling.

MUMMY'S BOY

Cries of "I want my mummy" took on a whole new twist recently when a man found himself stranded in a massage parlour without the necessary funds to secure his release. The man, aged 43, had been indulging himself in some vigorous one-on-one massage with a delightful masseuse by the name of Kelly Anne but found that he had left his wallet at home when it came time to pay. Kelly Anne called in her trained bodyguard and, between them, they were able to confirm that the man did indeed lack the necessary readies. They were, however, unwilling to let him go without paying and so he had to call his mother and get her to bring his wallet to the massage parlour.

SHORT CHANGED

Most of us are, no doubt, familiar with those shops, with names such as Happy Pics, which specialise in developing photographic films in under an hour. Many people may also have heard the stories about these stores keeping copies of picture of clients who were a little over exposed while on holiday. It is certainly true that these shops do a fine job of keeping an eye out for anything that might go beyond the bounds of good taste, especially when pictures turn up that may well be illegal. So it was that a shop recently called in the police after they developed a film that appeared to show a number of naked women cavorting with an obviously underage boy. Police confiscated the pictures and then lay in wait for their owner to collect them. Imagine the red faces when a 23-year-old dwarf turned up and asked if his pictures were ready.

PHOTO FINISH

At a large, well-attended wedding reception, the groom rose to express his thanks to all for turning up, and especially to the bride's parents for putting on such a fine (and expensive) spread. He thanked all the guests for their presents and offered, in return, a small gift which each of them would find under his or her seat. The guests reached down and found, taped to the bottom of their chairs, a small brown envelope. The groom waited while the guests opened the envelopes and held a blank expression on his face as they discovered, to their surprise, a recently-taken explicit photograph of the bride and the best man having sex. Then, barely pausing for breath, he bid everyone goodbye and went off to get the marriage annulled.

PHONE SEX

A woman in South West England called the police after receiving two phone calls in the early hours of the morning. Dismissing the first as an obscene call, she became alarmed when she heard what was clearly the sound of her daughter in some considerable state of distress. Along with the sound of a man's voice, she heard her daughter cry out "Oh my God" several times before the line went dead. The police rushed round to the daughter's house only to discover that she had been indulging in passionate sex with her boyfriend, who had been bashing the autodial button on her mobile phone with his toe.

PREMATURE ABSOLUTION

A Catholic priest in Chicago has been formally charged with the sexual abuse of a number of his parishioners. During questioning, the priest admitted to abusing his position as confidant and counsellor to the women of his parish by having sex with at least a dozen of them over a 20-year period. Offering a wonderful insight into the mind of a man who considered himself morally fit to absolve others of their sins, the priest added in mitigation that he was aware that his actions were both wrong and sinful. He explained that he always made an effort to get things over with quickly so that he could go and beg God for forgiveness.

BUSTY DEMISE

A 29-year-old man from Pennsylvania died while enjoying an evening's entertainment at his local strip club. Having first been to an ordinary bar to meet his friends, John "Boy" Boyman, moved on to the club where he was fortunate enough to secure a table at the front of the stage. The evening was going splendidly until Mr Boyman took it on himself to join in with one of the acts, a delightful former Sunday-school teacher working under the improbably name of Cherri Blossom. Noticing that despite having removed her bra, she was still hiding her modesty with a couple of sequined patches, Mr Boyman jumped on to the stage and attempted to remove them with his teeth. His attempt on the first patch was highly successful and so, emboldened by this, he attempted to chew off the other one. Unfortunately, he inhaled while doing so and choked to death on the patch.

PHOTO-GENITALS

An interesting, if not entirely convincing, excuse was offered in court in Edmonton, a suburb of London, England by a man who was charged with sending obscene material via Her Majesty's Royal Mail. The "material" in question was a Polaroid photograph of his genitals displayed in all their glory. The unfortunate recipient of the photograph, a business woman who lived in the area, took the offending material to the police. Investigating officers had no difficulty in tracking down the photogenic man as he had taken the time and trouble to write his name, address and sexual preferences on the back of the photograph. In his defence, the man claimed that he had not intended to send the picture to the woman who received it, but to a sex contact magazine. He told the court that he believed the picture, combined with a description of his preferences, would greatly improve his chances of meeting what he called "the right woman".

A LITTLE EDUCATION...

The very wonderful Lenny Bruce once said, while satirizing American attitudes to depictions of sex: "You can't show that, they might go out and do it some day." More than 30 years after his warnings, the words have come back to haunt an extreme right-wing Republican called John Schmitz. While his daughter was growing up, he made a stand on sex education in schools, opposing its very existence and even going so far as to remove his daughter from any institution that dared to teach the subject. Despite this gap in her education, Schmitz's daughter grew up, went to college, became a schoolteacher and then became a mother. She ended up facing a prison sentence as a result of her pregnancy. The father of the child turned out to be one of the young boys in her class, and his father was far from pleased to have been made a grandfather while his son was still trying to master the basics of Maths and English, in between receiving practical sex education lessons.

METAL MRS

Anyone who has ever spent time on the Internet looking for information will have discovered very quickly that the world is a shockingly bizarre place. There are all kinds of people out there, many of them barely literate, who have access to the World Wide Web and are able to share the contents of their diseased minds with the rest of us. A US-based special-effects artist has certainly found this to be the case. He normally makes life-sized steel-framed mannequins for use in movies as body doubles, to be thrown under cars or blown out of buildings. When he gave four of the dolls female names, and advertised them for sale on the net, he discovered that he could charge at least $4,000 a time for them.

TESTING TIME

In Turkey five young girls committed suicide rather than be put through the ordeal of a virginity test – which is carried out at all state-run orphanages. As if losing one's parents was not bad enough, the girls are subjected to this ordeal as part of code of honour, the roots of which are Islamic. Apparently, it is not at all unusual and is often carried out by the parents of Muslim girls for whom their daughter's purity is considered to be of paramount importance. Virginity testing is supported by the government. Apparently, it is not unheard of for parents whose daughter have died accidentally to insist on the test being carried out on the corpse so that they can rest easy in their beds at night in the sure and certain knowledge that their daughter died a virgin.

NO SEX, NO DANCING...

Fundamentalists in Afghanistan have jailed ten men for the heinous crime of watching someone dance. While some people dance so badly that they almost warrant a criminal prosecution, being jailed for dancing does seem particularly severe. But that is fundamentalism for you – the same fundamentalism that led to a man in Tehran being sentenced to death for having sex with his girlfriend. And over in the Malaysian state of Kelantan – where the cinema lights stay on by order of the law in an effort to stop couples kissing each other during films – supermarket queues must now be divided according to gender in order to stop romance blossoming in the aisles.

KIND TO ANIMALS?

Anyone who fears that their partner might be unfaithful could do worse than to check out a new report from the psychology department of the University of Texas. As a result of interviews carried out with 107 couples (one or both of whom had been unfaithful), the department was able to draw up a list of recognized behaviours, all of which point to the possibility that someone might be unfaithful, either now or in the future. Rather alarmingly, these behavioural characteristics included arriving late for dinner parties, spending too much time in the bathroom, getting into debt and forgetting to turn lights off. The surest clue as to the fidelity of one's partner was revealed to be a tendency on the part of the faithless to laugh at injured animals.

GOT THEM LICKED

It cannot be easy when, after being deported from a country, you turn up at home far earlier than expected and are then asked to give an account of yourself. It would be fair to say that when Englishmen are deported, it tends to be for outrages carried out while under the influence of alcohol that sometimes involve violence. But imagine the embarrassment of 38-year-old Peter Koenings, who was deported back to his home country of Holland for persistently harassing women on a single bus route in Nottingham by climbing under the seats and sticking his tongue through the gap in the cushions.

COME AGAIN?

That British journal of all things medical, *The Lancet*, reported recently on a very distressing condition that was causing a 44-year-old woman to suffer greatly. According to a report in the journal, the woman underwent spontaneous multiple orgasms about once every two weeks, regardless of where she was or what she was doing. The report went on to say that the woman found the condition especially distressing because she had no idea when the orgasms were going to take place as they were completely out of her control. Doctors were eventually able to improve her condition by treating an abnormality in the right side of her brain with a medication normally reserved for epileptics.

THANKS MUM

In August of 1997, the world was saddened to hear of the death of Jeanne Calment, who at 122 had been the oldest woman alive. (She had met Van Gogh, whom she described as vile-tempered and ugly.) The title of "The World's Oldest Woman" then fell to Canadian born Marie-Louise Meilleur who, by comparison, was but a spring chicken, being a mere 116 years of age. When she was approached by the world's press she was initially a little taken aback but soon fell into the usual habit that most mothers develop, that of embarrassing the children. When asked how she spent her days at the retirement home where she lived, she replied that she usually filled her time by trying to find a girlfriend for her 81-year-old son, who is also a resident...

DEMANDING WIFE

A couple who had been married only four months found themselves the subject of a police complaint and investigation after a number of incidents that had been disturbing their neighbours in the evening. Things came to a head in more ways than one when the woman assaulted her husband with a frozen loaf of bread, inflicting a scalp wound that required 12 stitches. When the police inquired as to why she had attacked her husband (and not for the first time) it emerged that they had fallen out over sex. It seems that she was offended when her husband refused to have sex with her for a fifth time that evening as he was "feeling tired after working all day". She is now believed to be suing for divorce on the grounds that her husband's behaviour is unreasonable.

FAIR WARNING

The Food and Drug Administration (FDA) was forced to issue a warning after sales of an electric cattle prod soared when the company that produced it decided to repackage the device on advice from a marketing company. Having previously seen the device sell in its hundreds to the country's many cattle farmers (and, no doubt the odd sadist), the company sold nearly half a million of the cattle prods when they relaunched it as "The Stimulator", claiming – although never in print – that it could be used to relieve the symptoms of head aches, bad backs, period pains, nose bleeds and even influenza (well it would certainly take your mind off them). In the FDA's warning, it is now pointed out that in the opinion of the FDA the device, if purchased by the cattle-less, should be used for nothing more than lighting a gas barbecue with the sparks that are produced at the tip of the prod.

WEIGHT LIFTERS

Doctors at a clinic in Rome have been investigating the effects of various drugs on men suffering from impotence (although where they found any Italian men who would admit to such a condition is a mystery). One drug that was tried – by injection into the urethra – was found not only to cause an all-too-temporary rigidity in the Italian members, but also led to an equally brief but none-the-less impressive increase in penis size. Measurements of the rigidity of the penises was obtained by hanging weights off the erection, gradually increasing the load to see how much could be carried in this way. The maximum load managed by any of the patients was a creditable 2.2 pounds.

AIRBAGS WITH TASSELS

Growing up in the Northwest of England, one quickly gets used to the sight of towns with unusual sounding names, such as Eccles, Timperley or even Sale. None of these names compares with that of Eureka, which is to be found the state of California. The owners of the Tip Top Club in Eureka – a venue popular with the locals for its fine selection of wines and its even finer selection of topless dancers – has got round the problem of a new local ordinance forbidding the operation of strip clubs, by becoming a car showroom. Customers are invited to sit back in the vehicles and enjoy the accompanying light show and topless dancers while puzzling over whether to go for the three-year free credit deal or the two-year free insurance and driver's airbag option.